New Zealand!
New Zealand!

Home Thoughts

I do not dream of Sussex downs or
    quaint old England's quaint
    old towns —
I think of what may yet be seen in
    Johnsonville or Geraldine.

– Denis Glover

New Zealand! New Zealand!

In Praise of Kiwiana

STEPHEN BARNETT ★ RICHARD WOLFE

Hodder & Stoughton

AUCKLAND LONDON SYDNEY TORONTO

A Bookmakers Book

©1989 Stephen Barnett and Richard Wolfe

Excerpts © the sources acknowledged on p. 8
Illustrations © the sources acknowledged on p. 157

This arrangement © 1989 Bookmakers Design & Production Ltd,
PO BOX 67-074, MT EDEN, AUCKLAND, NEW ZEALAND

First published 1989 by Hodder and Stoughton Ltd,
VIEW ROAD, GLENFIELD, AUCKLAND
Reprinted 1990

ISBN 0 340 485817

Designed by Stephen Barnett/Bookmakers

Production by Stephen Barnett and Richard Wolfe

Typesetting by Typeset Graphics Ltd, Auckland

Printed by Kyodo-Shing Loong Pte Ltd, Singapore

Contents

Acknowledgements

The authors wish to express their gratitude to the following organisations and individuals for encouragement, information, and making available various textual and pictorial materials. A detailed illustrations list appears on p. 157.

A Ministry of Agriculture and Fisheries; Air New Zealand; Alexander Turnbull Library Photographic Section (Joan McCracken, John Sullivan); Auckland City Art Gallery; Auckland Consul, Zephyr and Zodiac Car Club Inc. (Tony Lydford); Auckland Institute and Museum; Auckland Joggers Club; Auckland Observatory; **B** Murray and Pam Ball; Arthur Baysting; Bluebird Foods (Rosemary France); G. W. Broughton; Butland Industries Ltd (Geoff Polkinghorne); **C** Canterbury International (Mary Goodwin); Claude Neon (Peter Gray); Communicado (John Harris); Context (Alan Botica); Corbans Wines Ltd (Denis Robinson); Ron Cowell; Crown Lynn Potteries; **D** Ministry of Defence, Jenny Devine; John Devine; Dominion Breweries (John Miles); Dowse Art Museum; **E** Colin Edgerly; Department of Education; David Elworthy; *Evening Post*; **F** Farmers Trading Company; Ferndale Dairies; Fleming & Co. Ltd; Fisher & Paykel (Sue White); Foodstuffs NZ Ltd (Kevin Ferguson); Ford 8 & 10 Car Club; Ford Motor Company; Bruce Foster; **G** General Assembly Library; General Motors; Givani Footwear; Dave Gunson; **H** Mr and Mrs Hanlon; Hawes and Freer Ltd (Trevor Hookway); Department of Health (Elizabeth Macauley); Jim Henderson; Heylen Research Company (Vicki Hamilton); Michael Holroyd; **I** Department of Internal Affairs; International Rugby Museum; **K** Kiwi Pacific Records Ltd (Murray Vincent and Tony Vercoe); **L** Stephen La Plant; K. T. Lawson Group (Keith Lawson); Geoff Lealand; **M** Bruce and Michelle McLuckie; Masport NZ Ltd (Clive Blake and Murray Keyes); David Mealing; Keith Money; Mrs Mary More-Carter; Rod Morris; Morris Minor Car Club (Julie Hunt); **N** National Library; National Museum; National Tobacco Co.; NZ Co-operative Dairy Company Ltd; *NZ Herald*; NZ Kiwifruit Authority; NZ Marching Association; NZ Netball Association Inc.; NZ Patent Office; NZ Post; NZ Returned Servicemen's Association; Nicholas Kiwi; **O** Oasis Industries (Monique Tooley); **P** Paeroa Borough Council; Ron Palenski; Jock Phillips; **R** Radio Hauraki; Joan and Joyce Ramsey; Reckitt & Coleman Ltd; Reese Bros Plastics Ltd (Murray Limmer); Neil Rennie; Reserve Bank of NZ; Royal NZ Plunket Society; *Rugby Press;* H. J. Ryan Ltd (Bob Ryan); **S** Kath Salter; Sanitarium Health Foods (Lisle Burton); Department of Scientific and Industrial Research, Geophysics Department; Grant Sheehan; Wayne Smith; Department of Statistics; Jim Sullivan; Laurie Summers Accessories Ltd (David Ridge); Sunbeam Corp. (Victa Division); Swanndri Ltd (Warren Davis and Carl Webster); **T** Jeff Thomson; Paul Thompson; Tip Top Ice Cream Company Ltd (Margaret Stapleton); Totalisator Agency Board; Ministry of Transport; TVNZ; **U** Underwood Engineering (John Underwood); Unilever NZ Ltd (Richard Jeffrey); **W** Arthur Warnock; Philip Warren; J. Wattie Foods Ltd (Rex Linton); J. H. Whittaker & Sons Ltd; **Y** Yates NZ Ltd (Margaret McKee); Barry Young.

In addition, acknowledgement is made to the following for their kind permission to reproduce various excerpts. To *Belle* magazine for the extract from Robin Ingram's article on the backyard (pp. 64–66); Bluebird Foods for the hokey-pokey recipe (p. 47); Kiwi Pacific Records Ltd for the lyrics to Peter Cape's song 'Taumarunui' (p. 135); David McGill for his description of the six o'clock swill (p. 111); Keith Money for his description of Pavlova, and pavlova (p. 131); *North and South* magazine for the extract from a 'My Home Town' article by Lindsay Yeo (p. 129); Richards Literary Agency for the poem by Denis Glover (p. 3); Department of Scientific and Industrial Research, Geophysics Department, for the Mercalli Intensity Scale (p. 25); and to Geoffrey Short for his description of the Hutton's kiwis (p. 16).

For assistance with the design and production of the book, a big 'thank-you' to Jan Chilwell, Marilyn Gravette, Graeme Leather, Elinor McEwen, Tony Mack and Chris O'Brien.

And, for their suggestions and support, Christine Brown, Richard King and Phillip Ridge.

Preface

As the world grows smaller, national identities blur under an overlay of Western consumer culture. Fortunately there is an equal and opposite reaction that sees a growing concern for traditional folklore and imagery. It is to celebrate Kiwiana, the New Zealand 'difference', that this book has been compiled.

In the case of Kiwiana, not all of it has survived the global-villagising influences of television, travel and urbanisation, but recent years have seen an increasing interest in conserving what's left.

By and large, the bits and pieces that go to make up New Zealand's popular life and customs are pretty robust — the sheer isolation of the country saw to that. The early settlers, both Polynesian and Pakeha, had only what they brought with them: anything else they had to make themselves. Independence and resilience were traits necessary for survival.

Unlike many other colonised peoples, the indigenous Maori quickly adapted to the British way of life. The resulting mix of cultures inevitably deferred to the technological superiority of the latter, but common to both groups was work, recreation and mateship. The business of living was soon, unconsciously, forging a national identity.

The first 60 years of this century were characterised by a consolidation of popular culture, all the more so in the increasingly prosperous years following the end of the Second World War. For the baby-boom generation the quarter-acre section spread like a rash across freshly scraped hills. New roads sprang up to accommodate the Minors, Prefects, Vanguards and Veloxes. For the New Zealand bloke and his sheila and obligatory 2.6 kids there was also Plunket, Buzzy Bees, Saturday rugby and an occasional pav. And perhaps, now and then a bach in which to get away from it all.

New Zealand! New Zealand! is a fond remembrance of all that. If it tends to linger over the 1950s and 1960s then it is simply because this period spanned the authors' formative years, their earliest memories. As well, those halcyon days were ones in which New Zealand was often in the limelight. Our compatriots not only knocked off the world's highest mountain, but they also established an awesome reputation on the rugby field. Less noticed by the outside world were all the details in between. While this book can be no more than a selective lucky-dip into our popular culture, it will convey to the reader the strong sense of national identity that we feel is an integral part of the everyday and the commonplace.

In recording for posterity the aspects of Kiwiana contained herein, we realised there was a certain urgency. The availability of much of the material and access to prime sources was likely to become considerably more problematic with any further passage of time: mergers and takeovers can often result in a reduced regard for business archives, while the 'user-pays' mentality in government has resulted now and then in a lower priority being given to public access to records.

We were, however, fortunate in meeting with an enthusiastic and practical response to our research.

New Zealand! New Zealand! would have been impossible without the help of a multitude of individuals, companies and organisations. Our thanks to all of you, the makers and the keepers of our popular heritage, from Buzzy Bee to Weet-Bix.

STEPHEN BARNETT
RICHARD WOLFE
Auckland, 1989

Kia-Ora from New Zealand

New Zealand. Aotearoa. Just exactly who and what we think we are, and where we are going, are questions which have frequently taxed the national mind in recent years. As the country clocks over a mere century and a half of joint Maori-European society, it's probably a bit early, by several hundred years, for any concise and exact answers. However, there has been enough time, certainly, for a great many traditions, images and customs to have become firmly set in the collective memory and for the evolution of characteristics that mark the New Zealander.

Haere Mai, God Defend, silver fern,
kowhai, Southern Cross,
sheep and mates

Many are obvious and familiar, such as a passion for sport and the outdoors, while others are less tangible. But they are all byproducts of our response to life in our far-flung home.

Inhabiting a narrow stretch of land that looks like a small comma on a page that is the broad Pacific Ocean, New Zealanders have, like their fauna and flora, been shaped by geographical isolation. Both the Maori colonisers and the European settlers came ashore to an amazing land that nothing could have prepared them for: a place of strange and unfamiliar animals and plants in primeval settings.

Plunket, Anzacs, corrugated iron,
Swanndris, gumboots, marching girls,
meat pies, Sure to Rise and beer

There began an evolution of a popular life that suffered few severe shocks until the 1960s. Then, like every other Western country, New Zealand found itself in the throes of fundamental sociological and technological changes. Nothing was ever quite the same again.

Looking back at the early years of that decade — pre-EEC, pre-metric, pre-Vietnam — is much like reading Bruce Mason's *End of the Golden Weather:* ahead lay the cold winds of international economics, social divisiveness, the realisation that Manila is closer than Manchester. Between then and now the world changed, and so did we. However, while the New Zealand of then and the New Zealand of today appear in some respects as wholly different countries, in many others we continue to inhabit the New Zealand, both mythical and real, we remember.

Mt Cook, Tip Top, hokey pokey,
she'll be right, All Blacks, baches and beaut

Cowpat

Patriots

Cowpat patriots

UK delivery truck, 1930s.

New Zealanders are undoubtedly the only nation group whose colloquial identity has been consolidated by a brand of shoe polish. In the early years of European settlement a variety of symbols — predominantly the moa, silver fern, Southern Cross and kiwi — were used to represent the new nation and even by the early 1900s there still wasn't a clear consensus. The silver fern and Southern Cross enjoyed official recognition but the kiwi enjoyed popular appeal, a popularity that was soon to be enhanced by the success of an Australian shoe polish company.

When in 1906 William Ramsay developed a new shoe polish, he named it 'Kiwi' in honour of his wife's country of birth. The kiwi had the additional benefit of being an attractive and conveniently rounded image suited to a polish tin and, as well, the name is one that is easily read and pronounced in most languages. In 1914 the advent of the First World War saw a huge demand for polish for the millions of men under arms — leather booted and belted — and for horses' tack. Ramsay's polish, which had developed a reputation for a quality, deep, long-lasting shine, was the subject of huge orders from both British and US forces.

The transference of 'Kiwi' from its shoe polish association to First World War New Zealand soldiers was a simple matter. It was a connection further reinforced by the continuing success of Kiwi polish in postwar markets. Following the Second World War 'Kiwi' came to be synonymous with New Zealanders in general, not just those under arms. (And the shoe polish *was* to be found just about everywhere troops ventured. The American correspondent Walter Graeber wrote for *TIME* from the Tobruk trenches in 1942 that 'old tins of British-made Kiwi polish lay side by side with empty bottles of Chianti'.)

Oddly enough the kiwi has never received official recognition or legal protection as the emblem of New Zealand.

The kiwi bird itself is of course one of the wonders of this country's fauna. New Zealand's long geographical isolation, which occurred before the arrival of browsing and predatory mammals in this part of the Gondwanaland super-continent, resulted in a unique environment. Among its special features

THE
QUALITY
POLISH

MAKES A SHOE SHOW

The legs say it all.

'Kiwi' Keith, or more properly Keith Jacka Holyoake, was the country's prime minister throughout the prosperous sixties. As much as anything the 'Kiwi' prefix came to reflect the mateyness of the country during this decade and a desire to bring the lofty heights of statesmanship closer to the ordinary bloke and sheila. In fact, the nickname originated

A New Zealand duet: 'Kiwi' Keith and TT2.

from the man's childhood when he was known as 'Kiwi' Holyoake. While his decidedly un-Kiwi plummy voice and his pompousness could be diverting, he was a popular PM who visibly enjoyed the job. Apart from his dragging New Zealand into the Vietnam War, and the inability of his government to grapple with the implications of Britain's entry into the EEC, his tenure can be described as mostly harmless.

North Island brown kiwi.

Cowpat patriots

New Zealand servicemen stationed at Sling Camp in England during the First World War saw the chalk hill above the camp as a suitable site for the national emblem and proceeded to carve a giant kiwi into the hill. At 600 feet by 335 feet it was probably the largest kiwi image ever made.

'. . . a distinctive national identity.'

Trademark kiwis

was the evolution of a number of flightless and ground-dwelling bird species that adapted themselves to ecological niches that would elsewhere on Earth have been filled by mammals.

Best known of the ground-dwelling avifauna are the kiwis, survivors of an offshoot of an evolutionary line that included the now extinct moa. Flightless for thousands of years, the kiwi has only remnant wings hidden under a shaggy, hair-like plumage. Other unusual characteristics include a long bill that has the nostrils at the tip rather than at the base, as in the case of all other birds. In short, then, a unique animal.

Along with the silver fern and moa, the kiwi was used by European colonists to identify themselves with their new land and, while never given any official

recognition the kiwi was, and continues, nevertheless a popular emblem. As with the kiwi bird, our geographical isolation has set us apart as original products of a small and now mature nation. Conditions in other colonies may have been similar, but the New Zealand experience was more intensive. Taming the land and achieving recognition were self-imposed challenges that tested the nation's mettle.

During the last couple of decades the largest and most visible examples of the kiwi in commerce have been the big birds advertising Hutton's Kiwi Bacon factories. The kiwis and their accompanying neon signs were designed by Harry Rouse, designer with Claude Neon, and made by that firm. They were installed during the early to late 1960s.

Mounted atop buildings in Auckland, Christchurch, Wellington, Palmerston North, the steel and fibreglass kiwis at first rotated, but in later years when the turning gear broke down and proved immensely costly to repair they were anchored in one position. They became much-loved landmarks on the skylines of their cities, but in recent times as Huttons has rationalised its business the kiwis have been removed one by one. The last was the Auckland bird which until mid 1989 presided benignly over Kingsland. The kiwis were classic advertising sculptures which Auckland photographer Geoffrey Short has described as, 'so long part of their local environment that only strangers would think it odd that somehow kiwis might be a source of bacon'.

'Much-loved landmarks on the skylines of their cities...' the Kingsland, Auckland, Kiwi Bacon sign.

Cowpat patriots

New Zealand trench warfare — First World War.

*I*n Flanders' fields the poppies grow / Beneath the crosses row on row (Colonel McRae)

The red poppy of Flanders Fields was adopted in 1921 by the New Zealand Returned Soldiers' Association as the memorial flower of First World War dead. Emblematic of the fields on which were fought some of the cruellest campaigns in history, the image of the poppy was first used by the French Committee of the Children established at the end of the war to aid child victims of the fighting and of want. Along with other returned services' associations in the United Kingdom, the United States, Australia and Canada, the New Zealand RSA agreed to the wearing of the poppy in memory of the fallen. At first commemorative flowers were made by French orphans and widows and shipped to the various countries.

The original poppies had fabric petals and a fabric-covered wire stem, but in recent years these have been replaced by moulded plastic poppies.

Once worn on Armistice Day, 11 November, in New Zealand the poppy is today sold in the week prior to Anzac Day (April 25), a date with special meaning for us.

Of course the Gallipoli campaign, once seen as an uncomplicated set-piece of wartime sacrifice, has in recent years been reappraised as a monumental tragedy for which British command was knowingly culpable. Like lambs to the slaughter the soldiers of the Australia and New Zealand Army Corps (ANZAC) were thrown on to a small curve of beach under steep cliffs. Against any reasonable odds they were expected to not only knock out Turkish positions at the top of the cliffs and the high ground beyond, but also to cross the Gallipoli Peninsula and immobilise Turkish forts on the Dardanelle Straits.

In the first three days of the April 1915 landings 900 Kiwis were killed. Eight months later when the remnants of the Anzac force were evacuated the total was more than 2700 killed and many thousands more wounded. It was a scandalous military error of such proportions that only by elevating it to some kind of 'glorious death' could the military and political establishment expect a tolerable response from a grieving nation at home.

If our National Library is arguably the pinnacle of New Zealand's recorded heritage then it is appropriate that its postal address should be equivalent to the height, in feet, of the country's highest mountain. As pre-metricators will remember, this was the very easily remembered 12,349. Following metrication, Mt Cook's summit is a somewhat less impressive-sounding 3764 metres. Known to the Maori as Aorangi, the Cloud Piercer, the mountain was given its English name by Captain John Stakes of HMS *Acheron* in 1851 in honour of his navigator James Cook (not *the* James Cook, another one). It was first climbed on Christmas Day 1894 by Tom Fyfe, George Graham and Jack Clarke. Freda du Faur, an Austrian climber, became, in 1910, the first woman to reach the top.

'God Defend New Zealand', that slightly insecure invocation to the Almighty that has been our national hymn for the last half century, was written by Thomas Bracken in the 1870s. Bracken was the country's first popular poet, a flamboyant liberal who had arrived in New Zealand from Ireland via Australia where he'd worked as a stationhand, shearer, stock rider and prospector.

Settling in Dunedin Bracken was soon producing verse and prose that displayed both his pride in New Zealand and his concern for the rights of workers. He coined the phrase 'God's Own Country' in a poem of the same name:

> Give me, give me God's own
> country! there to live and
> there to die;

God's own country! fairest region resting 'neath the southern sky ...

Its publication gave the expression currency, although it is more frequently encountered today in the irreverent contraction 'Godzone'.

'God Defend . . .' first appeared in 1875 as a poem in the *Saturday Advertiser* which was edited by Bracken. A competition inviting a musical score for the poem was won by John Woods and in 1940 the song was officially adopted as our national anthem.

'God Save the Queen' is sung only infrequently these days but it is a mere generation ago that audiences at the start of theatre, opera and movie performances were obliged to stand for 'God Save' — in the case of the movies, the music accompanied by footage of HRH inspecting her guards at the 'Trooping of the Colour' or some such. The practice of standing lasted through to the late 1960s, disappearing first, earlier in that decade, from 'arty' cinemas like the Lido in Auckland where it had become the trend to remain firmly seated.

> *God of Nations, at thy feet,*
> *In the bonds of love we meet,*
> *Hear our voices we entreat,*
> *God defend our Free Land.*
> *Guard Pacific's triple star*
> *From the shafts of strife and war,*
> *Make her praises heard afar,*
> *God defend New Zealand.*
> (First verse)

Cowpat patriots

*N*ew Zealand's first attempt at a Coat of Arms paralleled moves away from colonial status and towards being a Dominion. A competition for a design, promoted in the early 1900s, drew numerous entries. Among the many depicting kiwis, cows, moas and sheep was one by James McDonald, a draughtsman in the Department of Tourism and Health Resorts, and which, after modification, was adopted.

In 1956 Queen Elizabeth II gave approval to a revised version of the Arms. The motto 'Onward' was replaced with the name 'New Zealand' on a scroll of two fern leaves and the supporters were made to face inwards, the Maori chieftain losing his hei tiki and gaining a kapeu — greenstone ear pendant — which was considered to be a more appropriate ornament.

The first quarter of the shield depicts four stars representing the Southern Cross (similar to those on the New Zealand flag). The golden fleece, the wheat sheaf and miners' implements represent early European industries and make up the remaining three-quarters of the shield. The two halves of the shield represent the North and South islands separated by a vertical stripe for Cook Strait, with three symbolic ships to typify the importance of our sea trade.

Above the shield is St Edward's Crown which was used in the coronation ceremony of Queen Elizabeth II.

As we approach the twenty-first century, there is still debate over what should constitute a proper national symbol. Kiwis we may be, and the kiwi

Silver Fern

A predominant feature of the New Zealand bush are the ferns, indeed an early colloquial name for the country was Fernland. The tallest of these is the tree fern or ponga, and it is the leaf of this species that is one of our best-known national symbols. From the very beginning of European settlement the fernleaf found its way on to newspaper mastheads and into advertising. Later it came to be incorporated into military and sports badges.

an internationally recognised symbol, but equally well known to foreigners is the silver fern. The image that marks our dairy product exports, the fernleaf, first appeared on the badge of the New Zealand Native rugby team that toured Britain in 1888. It has been used — a silver or white fern design on black ground — as the country's sporting emblem ever since.

In addition, fernleaves distinguished New Zealand's armed services in both the world wars, and in 1956 the silver fern was incorporated into the revised Coat of Arms. However, the popularisation of the term 'Kiwi' by both the shoe polish and the subtropical fruit has given new emphasis to the kiwi bird as a national emblem. (And this despite the fact that, for millions of Europeans

at least, the 'kiwi' — their shorthand for kiwifruit — is something you eat.)

Then there is the Southern Cross, another popularly used image which on the New Zealand flag is difficult even for New Zealanders to distinguish from the Australian version. Curiously enough, only the Southern Cross enjoys any sort of legal protection in its use as an emblem of this country. . .and then only to the extent of its depiction on the flag. As for the kiwi and the silver fern, neither is protected by statute. Worse, it is not illegal to use these symbols to *misrepresent* goods as being of New Zealand origin! None of the symbols are government marks, an omission that must be risky at the present time when competition for brands and market is intense.

'. . .the country's sporting emblem since 1888.'

Cowpat patriots

T he British settlers who made up the great majority of European immigrants to New Zealand brought with them a deep loyalty to Britain and to the monarchy. Indeed it was a strength of feeling that inspired the epithet 'Britain of the South Seas' for New Zealand, and which saw Kiwis at the forefront of any call for arms, from the South African veldts of the Boer War to Monte Cassino. 'Where [Britain] goes, we go, where she stands, we stand', as Michael Joseph Savage said in 1939 at the outbreak of the Second World War.

Despite the fact that Britain as 'Home' was of diminishing relevance to New Zealanders in the postwar years, the national blood still ran red-white-and-blue. Visits by any member of the Royal Family were major events which pulled

Kiwis three and four deep to watch the royal procession. And none more so than the 1953-54 visit by Queen Elizabeth II. It was the first visit to these shores by a reigning monarch. HRH had been crowned earlier in 1953 following the death of her father George VI, and it had been a coronation in which this country enjoyed some reflected glory with the announcement, on the day of the coronation, that the world's highest mountain had been conquered for the first time a few days before, by a New Zealander, Edmund Hillary.

The royal tour — a big one, 39 days, 56 towns and cities, Dargaville to Bluff — totally captivated public attention. From their arrival in Auckland — to a welcome from 100,000 people — to their departure, the royal guests were fêted

continually. Later tours never quite repeated the same huge expression of goodwill and interest, but our feelings towards British royalty remain at least benign, with many New Zealanders continuing to possess some admiration if not a little awe for the woman who personifies the monarchy.

In the 1830s, when New Zealand-built ships first began to cross the Tasman to trade with Australia, they did so without the benefit of a national register. Customs regulations required trading vessels to have a national ensign and with this incentive some urgency was given to the design of a New Zealand flag.

The first attempt, by naval authorities in New South Wales — which colony was at that time responsible for governing New Zealand — was rejected here because it was lacking in red, the colour which to the Maori signifies rank. Alternatives were run up in Sydney and sped over to Waitangi on HMS *Alligator*. On 20 March, 1834, 30 Maori chiefs gathered to make their choice and selected a design involving two red crosses on a white ground accompanied by four eight-pointed stars. Known as the 'Flag of the Independent Tribes' this flag flew in New Zealand until 1840, when it was supplanted by the Union Jack.

St George may have inspired the two red crosses of the Flag of the Independent Tribes, but the origin of the stars is not so clear. It is more likely that they represented the four countries of the United Kingdom than the four brightest members of the Southern Cross. Later, however, the Southern Cross was recognised when, in 1869, it was incorporated into the maritime blue ensign.

The remaining years of the 19th century saw a growing public affection for the blue ensign as a more suitable flag for New Zealand. It was increasingly flown on land as well as at sea and in 1902 it was officially adopted as the national flag.

Cowpat patriots

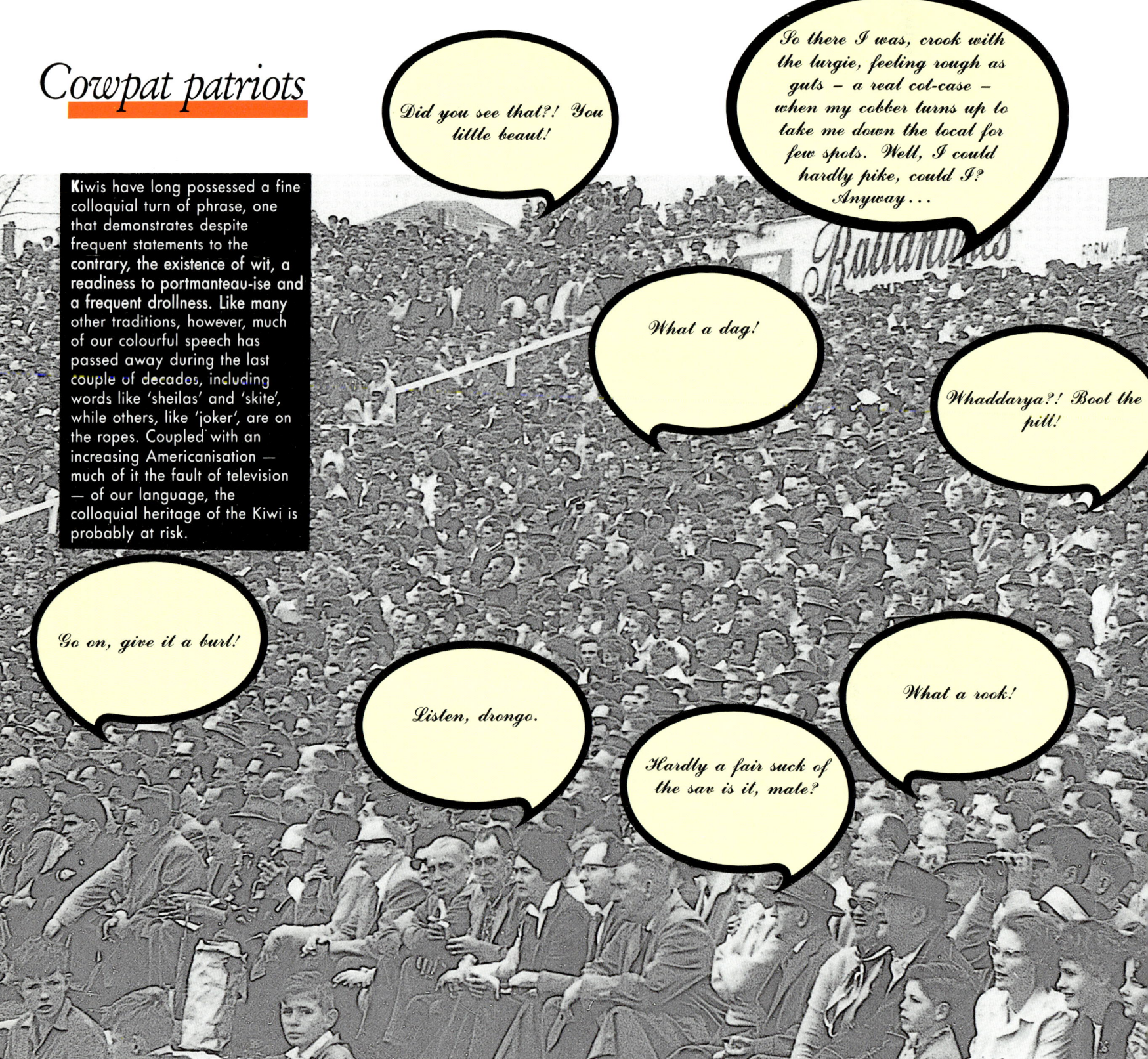

Kiwis have long possessed a fine colloquial turn of phrase, one that demonstrates despite frequent statements to the contrary, the existence of wit, a readiness to portmanteau-ise and a frequent drollness. Like many other traditions, however, much of our colourful speech has passed away during the last couple of decades, including words like 'sheilas' and 'skite', while others, like 'joker', are on the ropes. Coupled with an increasing Americanisation — much of it the fault of television — of our language, the colloquial heritage of the Kiwi is probably at risk.

Modified Mercalli Intensity Scale

Masonry A, B, C, D
To avoid ambiguity of language, the quality of masonry brick or otherwise is specified by the following lettering:

Masonry A
Good workmanship, mortar and design; reinforced, especially laterally, and bound together by using steel, concrete, etc.; designed to resist lateral forces.

Masonry B
Good workmanship and mortar; reinforced, but not designed in detail to resist lateral forces.

Masonry C
Ordinary workmanship and mortar; no extreme weakness like failing to tie in at corners, but neither reinforced nor designed against horizontal forces.

Masonry D
Weak materials, such as adobe; poor mortar; low standards of workmanship; weak horizontally.

Intensity Scale
I. Not felt. Marginal and long-period effects of large earthquakes.

II. Felt by persons at rest, on upper floors, or favourably placed.

III. Felt indoors. Hanging objects swing. Vibration like passing of light trucks. Duration estimated. May not be recognised as an earthquake.

IV. Hanging objects swing. Vibration like passing of heavy trucks; or sensation of a jolt like a heavy ball striking the walls. Standing motor cars rock. Windows, dishes, doors rattle. Glasses clink. Crockery clashes. In the upper range of IV, wooden walls and frame creak.

V. Felt outdoors; direction estimated. Sleepers wakened. Liquids disturbed, some spilled. Small unstable objects displaced or upset. Doors swing, close, open. Shutters, pictures move. Pendulum clocks stop, start, change rate.

VI. Felt by all. Many frightened and run outdoors. People walk unsteadily. Windows, dishes, glassware broken. Knick-knacks, books, etc. off shelves. Pictures off walls. Furniture moved or overturned. Weak plaster and masonry D cracked. Small bells ring (church, school). Trees, bushes shaken.

VII. Difficult to stand. Noticed by drivers of motor cars. Hanging objects quiver. Furniture broken. Damage to masonry D, including cracks. Weak chimneys broken at roof line. Fall of plaster, loose bricks, stones, tiles, cornices. Some cracks in masonry C. Waves on ponds; water turbid with mud. Small slides and caving in along sand or gravel banks. Large bells ring. Concrete irrigation ditches damaged.

VIII. Steering of motor cars affected. Damage to masonry C; partial collapse. Some damage to masonry B; none to masonry A. Fall of stucco and some masonry walls. Twisting, fall of chimneys, factory stacks, monuments, towers, elevated tanks.

In a country in which volcanic and seismic activity has been a sizable feature of the geology, perceivable earthquakes are a frequent occurrence. Many of the inhabitants, notably in Wellington, have grown accustomed to the rattle of teacups and the swing of suspended objects.

While the best known measurement is of earthquake size — Richter magnitude — a measure of what damage is caused and how badly you get shaken is more pertinent.

Severity of ground shaking depends not only on the magnitude but also on how close you happen to be to the centre of the shock. Some earthquakes occur at hundreds of kilometres under the ground at depths from which they may be felt but can generally cause little damage.

The measure of severity of shaking in an earthquake — called the intensity, which rates higher closer to the epicentre and lower further way — is the modified Mercalli Intensity scale.

Sometimes two distinct shakes are felt in an earthquake — often the first is not felt so much as heard, as a very low rumble — and it is possible by counting the time between them to calculate roughly how far from the earthquake's epicentre you are. Reckon on eight kilometres for every second between the two shakes.

Frame houses moved on foundations if not bolted down; loose panel walls thrown out. Decayed piling broken off. Branches broken from trees. Changes in flow or temperature of springs and wells. Cracks in wet ground and on steep slopes.

IX. General panic. Masonry D destroyed; masonry C heavily damaged, sometimes with complete collapse; masonry B seriously damaged. Frame structures, if not bolted, shifted off foundations. Frames racked. Serious damage to reservoirs. Underground pipes broken. Conspicuous cracks in ground. In alluviated areas sand and mud ejected, earthquake fountains, sand craters.

X. Most masonry and frame structures destroyed with their foundations. Some well-built wooden structures and bridges destroyed. Serious damage to dams, dikes, embankments. Large landslides. Water thrown on banks of canals, rivers, lakes, etc. Sand and mud shifted horizontally on beaches and flat land. Rails bent slightly.

XI. Rails bent greatly. Underground pipelines completely out of service.

XII. Damage nearly total. Large rock masses displaced. Lines of sight and level distorted. Objects thrown into the air.

From Karitane

to Kaput

From Karitane to kaput

Sir Truby King.

F or nearly as long as the country has been 'Godzone', New Zealand has also been hailed as a 'good place to bring up children'. If the saying became a cliché then it was only because it was a truth often stated. It was certainly the case from the 1940s on and, despite a sometimes fashionable cynicism to say otherwise, is still so today.

By the early 1940s New Zealand was at the forefront of care for the infant and child. Among other things this included free dental and medical schemes; free milk in schools; towns and cities free of the pressures of a crowded high-density population; unrestricted access to an abundance of fresh air, sunlight, and the wilderness of hills and coast.

Conventionally the New Zealand welfare system provided total care from the cradle to the grave. Following his or her birth in a state-funded hospital, the new Kiwi was taken under the wing of a Plunket nurse whose observations on baby's progress and height and weight were awaited with keen anticipation by the parents. A 'Plunket' baby was the goal of most.

Founded in 1907, at a time when the country's record on infant care was abysmal, the Plunket Society has become an integral part of the country's health system. More than that it is a part of the weave of our social fabric. It is an extraordinary example of just what a grass-roots people's movement can achieve: in the case of Plunket, a nationwide organisation of preventative care that has not only succeeded by influence and example rather than imposition, but has done so largely by a support network of volunteers. It is a system unique to this country.

It was while working as a medical superintendent in Dunedin that Dr Frederic Truby King became aware of the need for mothers to be better educated in the care of their babies. It was a popularly held belief of the time that mothers knew instinctively how to care for their children but the situation that existed in the early 1900s suggested otherwise. Bottle-feeding of babies had largely supplanted breast–feeding, with dire results in many cases. There was little knowledge of the preparation of nourishing and balanced formula milks and, instead, straight cows' milk or heavily sugared commercial preparations

That treasured icon of Kiwi parenthood, the Plunket book, was first issued in the 1920s. Like those that followed it, it included a chart to plot weight gains, and space for the Plunket nurse to write comments regarding the baby's attainments and care requirements. Two decades later, following a nationwide survey of 9000 Plunket babies, the books began to include growth-curve graphs as well. These matched age with desirable height and weight and, at a period when the Society was stressing strict adherence to Truby King's principles of infant care, any deviation, to below the mean line especially, resulted in some measure of parental anxiety. And was, no doubt, partly responsible for the term 'Plunket baby' coming to describe an infant who today would be regarded as overly bonny.

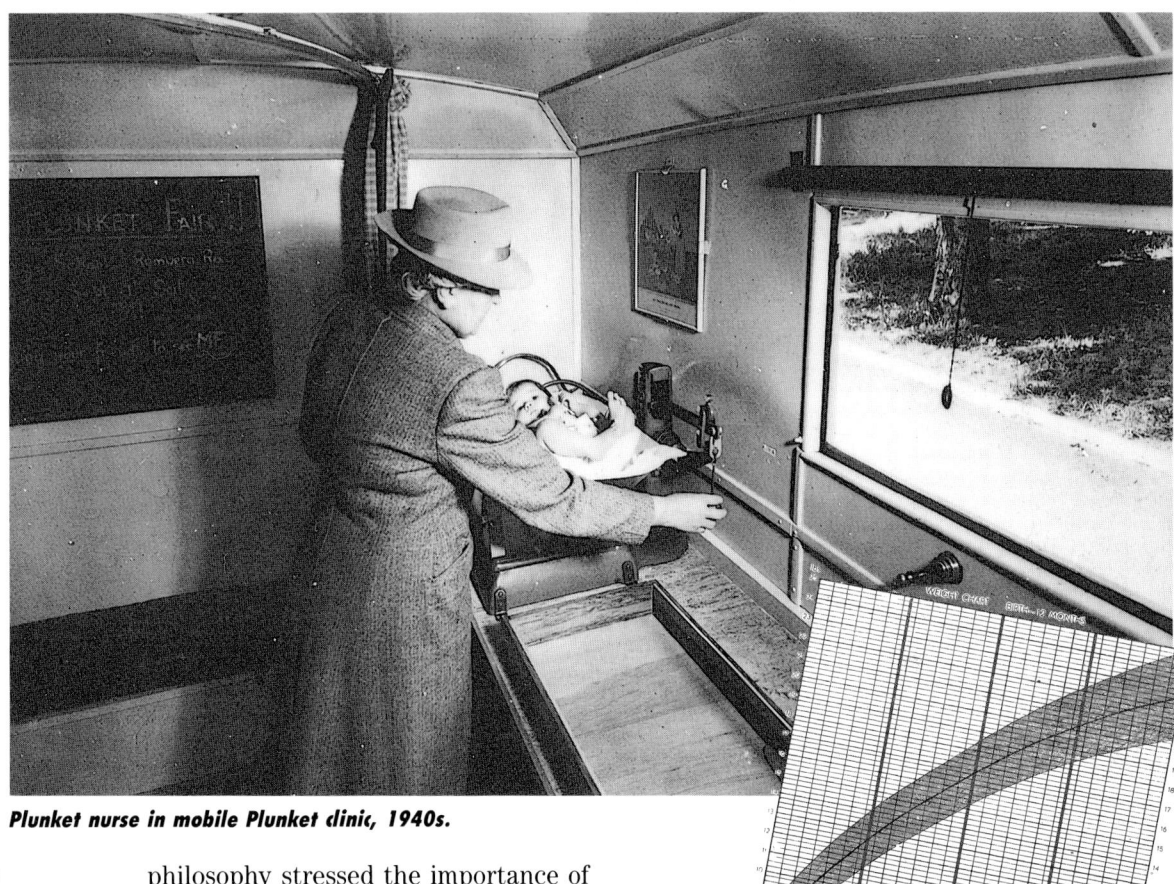

Plunket nurse in mobile Plunket clinic, 1940s.

were often given. The result was frequently severe digestive upset and a scandalously high infant mortality rate.

One of Truby King's first achievements was to devise a recipe for what he termed 'humanised milk': a formula preparation that supplied as near as possible the nutrients of mother's milk.

First founded as The New Zealand Society for the Health of Women and Children, the organisation later came to be called the Plunket Society, in recognition of the high-profile support given by Lady Plunket, wife of the governor-general. Vice-regal patronage gave the society a major boost and with Lady Plunket's assistance branches were established throughout the country.

As well as proper nutrition the King

philosophy stressed the importance of fresh air, sunshine, diet and exercise in the pursuit of the happy, healthy child. At first, the King cottage at the seaside suburb of Karitane was lent to the Society as a hospital for the care of malnourished and neglected children. Later, when the Society set up a new hospital in a larger residence in Dunedin, the seaside connection was carried on in its name — the Karitane Home for Babies, the first of a string of such hospitals. For 70 years Plunket and Karitane nurses trained at the Homes and went out to carry the King gospel to all parts of New Zealand.

By the 1980s the Karitane Homes had become uneconomic. They have all now been closed and in their place have opened Family Centres. These, along

with the Plunket rooms that are as much a part of New Zealand as the RSA halls, continue to extend Plunket care for the great majority — more than 85 percent — of all new Kiwis. Today's Plunket nurse, rather than laying down the law, is a friendly advisor whose professional health care is part of a system supported by both government and volunteers.

On his death Sir Truby King, as he'd become in recognition of his services, was accorded, quite properly, a state funeral.

From Karitane to kaput

1920s open-fronted classroom.

THE EGMONT EXERCISE BOOK

Pupil's Name *Rita Kavanagh*
Standard *IV* *English*
School *Convent High*

The first day at primary school represents for most children their first exposure to the demands of the adult world, arrived at after a five-year period of grace perhaps spent in sandpit and with blocks at Playcentre or one of the state kindergartens. Fortunately, that first introduction, via the primer classes, was, and still is, a gentle one.

In keeping with the trends that characterised pioneer welfare schemes in the early decades of this century, the line on education was that the time children spent within the halls of learning should be physically beneficial as well. So that, in a land of generally temperate climate and with space to spread out, primary schools would provide large areas of playing-fields and only single-storey, airy classrooms.

The first of our classic verandah-style primary schools was built in the Christchurch suburb of Fendalton, the large, glass folding doors that spanned one wall of each classroom designed to allow in the maximum of sunlight and fresh air, with the classrooms themselves facing out on to play areas. A civilised and thoughtful design, devised with a wish to marry rather than divorce the needs of learning from the outdoors, it remained the dominant one for all new schools built between the twenties and the mid-fifties.

The three R's in the fifties meant *Janet and John*, pounds, shillings and pence, stones and hundredweights, and long division. New maths and metrics belonged to a future generation. But it wasn't all schoolwork of course.

Lunchtime and morning and afternoon playtimes were given over to climbing on the Taranaki frame, games of tiggie, bullrush, or soccer played by teams of considerably more than the required eleven, patter tennis, or perhaps one of the then-current cyclic fads like marbles (steelies and glassies) or tops. In the older classes there might be a little emergent romancing as well.

The architecture of your typical fifties' and sixties' primary school possessed a number of distinctive features. The main administration building and classrooms were typically weatherboarded on the outside and tongue-and-groove inside, with sash windows — akin to traditional domestic house architecture of the 1920s. Spanning the windows of one outside wall would

'Look, John, look!' First readers for postwar primary schoolchildren were the *Janet and John* series. Originating in an American infant reader series which had been adapted for UK schools, *Janet and John* was a further adaptation in consultation with the New Zealand Department of Education. The series joined the *School Journal* and A.W.B. Powell's *Native Animals of New Zealand* as the most memorable of publications put before primary schoolchildren of that period.

In simple repetitive prose the *Janet and John* readers strove for the pupil's quickish acquisition of a reasonable vocabulary. Many teachers and educators eventually came to see them as over-emphasising vocabulary and because of this, and dissatisfaction with the quality of the stories and the

John, see the aeroplanes.
One, two, three aeroplanes.
I can see three aeroplanes.

20

John said,
"See the aeroplane go up.
See the aeroplane fly.
The aeroplane can fly fast.
Fly fast, big aeroplane."

21

nature of the characters involved, at the end of the fifties the series was wound down. It was replaced with the *Ready to Read* series of books.

be a board carrying the school motto, such as 'Sacrifice Before Self', whose influence was there any time pupils might care to raise their eyes, even if the strength of the message was perhaps a little diluted by the presence of extraneous straw and string and feathers protruding from behind the board, where sparrows nested warm and dry.

Somewhere near the entrance to the main block classrooms — perhaps in the corridor with its coathooks carrying brown leather schoolbags and a door leading off to the sick bay — would be the Honours Board. This carried the names of former pupils and teachers who had 'fallen' during the Great Wars. Imposing in scale and sombre in colour, this roll of honour and its legend that usually referred to some unsettling

concept such as the 'Glorious Dead', was a shadowy symbol of something bigger than a child's understanding. A something which the annual Anzac Day service with its singing of 'guarding Pacific's triple star from the shafts of strife and war' made little clearer. . . Sometime, somewhere, there'd been a battle in which lots of New Zealand soldiers had died (though not in vain) so that there was glory in defeat, and yet we had eventually won anyway. . .

If the school roll had risen substantially since the school had been opened (and, of course, as the children of the postwar baby boom reached school age, primary school rolls of the fifties leapt up) then the original classroom accommodation was added to by fibrolite pre-fabs.

Then there was the boilerhouse, the heart of a hotwater heating system that ended in rumbling and vibrating radiators along classroom walls; the shelter-shed, often doubling as the bike-shed but more usually the only place outside you could huddle on wet days; the dunnies (the boys' one open to the air above the urinal so that you were doubly concerned to avoid being wetted); and the Murder House.

Sited away some distance from all the other buildings, along a lonely pathway, the dental clinic crouched lying in wait for its young victims. Twice a year the dental nurse raised the pulse rates and adrenalin levels of her charges with a summons, her fateful messengers entering classrooms to quietly speak those words to the teacher that meant

From Karitane to kaput

School dental clinic, Palmerston North, 1950.

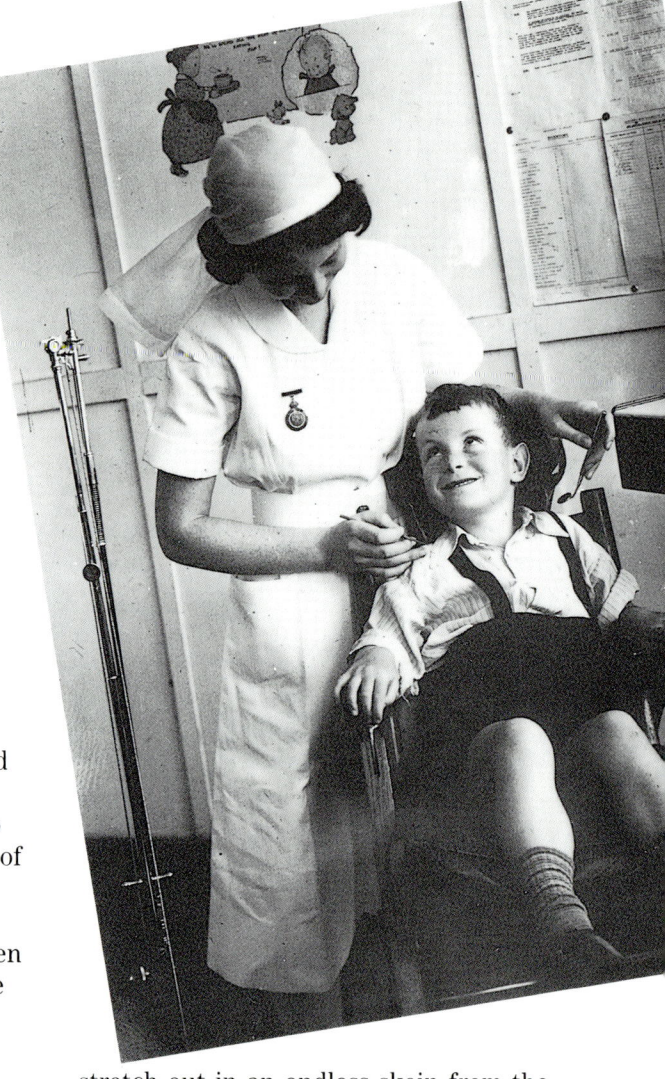

only one thing. But *who*?! The teacher's face would slowly scan the ordered rows of desks. . .

If you were *really* unlucky the electric drill would be out of action, or perhaps it was being used by a new graduate, and you'd get one of the old treadle machines whose effectiveness, not to mention painlessness, was dependent upon the dental nurse keeping a reasonable speed with her foot. A hot afternoon at the end of a week could make the visit an endurance. It wasn't until the early sixties that all treadle machines were replaced by electrically-driven ones.

Along with New Zealanders' general health, the state of their teeth in the early years of this century had also reached a low point — the result of poor dental hygiene and a shortage of dentists. An urgent remedy was needed and in contemplating a dental nurse scheme, the government didn't need to look any further than the attainments of the Plunket Society.

In the years since its inception in 1921, the School Dental Service has been enormously successful in improving the general oral health of young children. The scheme's emphasis on prevention and education — coupled with the claimed benefits of widespread fluoridation of public water supplies in these years — has resulted in a dramatic change in dental requirements. The subsequent decrease in the use of the drill is no doubt gratifying to today's schoolchildren.

While the school year seemed to stretch out in an endless skein from the late summer heat of February, relief was promised by the term holidays, the start of which, following tidying-up on the term's last day, was signalled by the cry of 'chairs on tables'. When it came for the last time at primary school at the end of the Form II year, the impending move to secondary school the next year

Victims entering the school 'murder house' were usually greeted first by the sight of 'propaganda' posters from the Dental Health Service. Some threatened dire consequences for those who ignored toothbrush drill, while others extolled the goodness, teethwise, of fruits, vegetables and milk. But the biggest single campaign was probably that surrounding 'Bertie Germ'. Cast in the shape of a mischievous elf (or elves: Bertie Germ was something of a collective singular) Bertie the Germ (again some flexibility here) was depicted as delighting in children's neglect of proper dental care. Cavities were the result. Against Bertie were ranged the forces of good in the form of silver fairies, toothbrush drill, raw fruits and veges and, of course, the dental nurse's drill. While its origin is vague — whether Bertie Germ was a local invention or instead a local adaptation of an overseas concept is unclear — he or they, appear to have been around since the 1930s.

Frames from a 1950 film strip featuring the Bertie Germ boys.

represented more than just going on to a new class. It was as well a coming of age, the summer break a transition from childhood to teenager.

Many of our great welfare institutions have resulted from the vision and drive of individuals, and this is certainly true of the founding of the health camp system. As with the Plunket Society and the school dental health scheme, the idea of health camps was a response to the largely poverty-related poor health visible in a huge number of New Zealanders in the early years of the 1900s.

During the 1920s, while serving as a school medical officer in Wanganui, Elizabeth Gunn came up with the idea of health camps to which sickly children could go to benefit from a health-promoting regime of fresh air, exercise and good food. Rather than treating poor health with purely medicines it was Elizabeth Gunn's assertion that a balanced health care programme — of which sunbathing with its beneficial vitamin D was a feature — was more important.

With the help of a local farmer, B.P. Lethbridge, Elizabeth Gunn opened the first camp near Wanganui. In the years immediately following, camps were also established in other parts of the country.

At first the camps had to rely on the resources of voluntary organisations but in 1929 they began to receive monies from the first health stamps issued by the Post Office. The stamps were, once again, the realisation of yet another personal campaign.

Drawing on her knowledge of the fund-raising Christmas seals used in her Danish homeland, Kristine Nielson of Norsewood suggested something similar here to fund the camps. After many years of lobbying the first stamp was released in 1929. Like all those produced to the present day, part of the cost of the stamp went to paying postage, and part to the health camps.

Early issues were memorable for their designs, such as the 'Keyhole' stamp and the triangular one of 1943 featuring the royal princesses. Child health has improved immeasurably in recent decades but seven camps still continue to offer children a healthy break away from home which they otherwise might not have.

From Karitane to kaput

The ten o'clock swill.

George Bernard Shaw made a big impact when he came to New Zealand in 1934. During his month-long stay here he drew crowds wherever he went and was listened to for his opinions on and criticisms of everything from school milk to tourism. Shaw, like many other social commentators of the time, saw New Zealand as a kind of social laboratory in which the absence of class, and the existance of an even spread of wealth, gentle climate and ready access to open spaces, was producing a fair and just society of fit and healthy individuals.

*F*or anyone at primary school from the late 1930s until the late 1960s, one of the most enduring memories is of the ritual of school milk. All across the country at 10 o'clock sharp the rattling of half-pint bottles in wire crates signalled morning playtime.

While the exact origins of the 10 o'clock swill are confused, there had been discussion during the Depression about matching the huge milk surplus from the dairy industry with the thousands of children undernourished as a result of the poverty of the times. A number of localised schemes distributing milk to schoolchildren were begun in such places as Wellington and Nelson in the early thirties, but it was in February 1937 that a nation-wide free-milk scheme, introduced by Labour Minister of Health and Education, Peter Fraser, began.

The various lobbyists that led to its adoption included George Bernard Shaw who, during a visit to New Zealand in 1934, gave a radio talk which included his thoughts on the matter:

You have in Wellington a remarkable milk supply, which is the envy of the whole world,' he said during this broadcast, 'but your milk I think costs too much. I just want to ask, why not distribute milk freely? That is very important in New Zealand.

'A little loss on milk does not matter. It is of enormous importance that all your children should have plenty of milk and that the next generation should be a generation reared from first-class children. When you have done this, when you have distributed free milk, which is just as possible as free water, I would then suggest that you should go on from free milk to free bread.'

Health Department annual reports from the 1920s had identified a range of health problems suffered by primary schoolchildren — from dental caries, deformities of the trunk and chest, enlarged tonsils and adenoids, and scrawniness — that could apparently be largely aided by a daily intake of milk.

It was an argument for beneficial health that dovetailed with the need for an extra home market for what was then the country's chief primary product. The scheme contributed to the raising of a couple of healthy generations of Kiwis until a National government ended it in 1967.

The first of the designs for the new decimal currency met with a small storm of controversy when they were released. Images such as a rugby player on the 20 cent coin and a musterer on the 50 cent were derided, and the Decimal Currency Board rapidly set about their replacements. The coins we use today are all the work of the late Wellington designer James Berry. The 1 cent and 2 cent coins proved to be the most popular, in a manner of speaking. Since 1967 nearly a billion of them have been minted but only a fraction of that number were ever in circulation. The rest presumably languish idle and uncared for at the backs of drawers, in old jars, down between settee cushions, and like places. Meantime the effects of inflation rendered their worth virtually meaningless and in 1989 they were abolished.

British coins were used in New Zealand up until 1933 when they were replaced by local coinage. The change was introduced mainly because of the variance in the exchange rates between the two countries, occasioned by devaluations of the New Zealand £ against the British £ in 1931 and 1933. This made it very profitable to smuggle British coin back to the United Kingdom and exchange it. When the first trading banks were established here they issued their own series of bank notes of varying sizes and designs. Eventually, the handling of six different lots of banknotes proved too much. In 1934 the Reserve Bank was established and given the sole right to issue notes.

*I*n the days when money had some real value, in the days of £sd (and before *that* took on a different connotation), £5 was a small fortune. And there are more than a few people who look back and consider there to have been some kind of connection between the advent of decimalisation and the beginnings of rampant inflation. Certainly today's $10 equivalent to the old 'fiver' probably buys even less than did a 'quid'. And that was another of the nice things about the old imperial system — currency had a more human face then, not only in the language of money, filled as it was with florins, bobs, shillings, half-crowns, tenners, zacs, tanners, thruppences and ha'p'neys, but also in its basis of relativity.

A pleasantly eccentric system of halves, quarters, twelfths and twentieths, it was a demanding one (especially its multiplication and division) but at least it had some character to it. And of course, even the lowliest of coins had real buying power then. They looked it — the halfpenny the size of a ten-cent piece, the penny as big as 50 cents.

Leaving aside for a minute the weightiness of even 1s 6d in pennies and halfpennies, the jangle of imperial coin was always impressive. That all came to an end on 10 July 1967 (and if you were around at the time you won't have forgotten the incessant promotion of the changeover, 'tenth of July next/this year!') when the more *sensible,* more *efficient* decimal alternative was introduced. Ten years later you could still meet older people in particular who

2 halfpence	**1** penny
3 pence	**1** threepenny-piece
4 threepenny-pieces	**1** shilling
6 pence	**1** sixpence
2 sixpence	**1** shilling (1s)
12 pence	**1** shilling
20 shillings	**1** pound (£1)
24 pence	**1** florin
10 florins	**1** pound
30 pence	**1** half-crown
8 half-crowns	**1** pound
2 crowns	**10** shillings
1 sovereign	**20** shillings

converted dollar and cent prices back to pounds in order to get an idea of an item's real value. And, curiously, more than 20 years after decimalisation the old imperial currency remains legal tender. You may get some funny looks when you bring out your crumpled up ten bob notes but they still count.

From Karitane to kaput

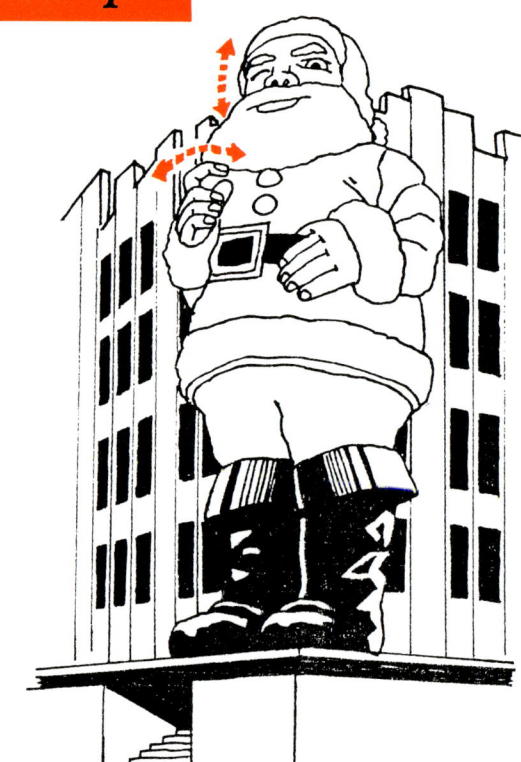

Christmas wasn't Christmas without the parades organised by the country's big department stores. Best-known were the annual Hays Christmas Parade, in Christchurch, and Farmers Trading Company Santa Parade in Auckland. The latter was and still is a magnet to families from all over the region ... and in the fifties a visit to Auckland wasn't complete without a ride on a Farmers escalator and, of course, gazing awestruck at the giant Santa figure adorning the outside of the famous Hobson Street store — the gent's winking eye and beckoning finger as much a personal greeting as an invitation to come inside the store.

A stalwart of school lunches and picnics are the triangular-shaped, smooth-textured, smokey-tasting cheese segments made by Chesdale. Deriving from a time when refrigeration was rare, Chesdale processed cheese had the virtue of keeping well. In contrast, ordinary cheese, particularly once it was cut, sweated, became oily, then dried out, cracked, grew mould, began to pong and crumbled. Perhaps even worse. Today Chesdale continues as a popular cheese and its advertising characters, Ches and Dale, have become something of a Kiwi tradition. Along with 'Broke My Dentures' and 'It Must Be Watties' the famous Chesdale jingle is almost part of New Zealand folklore.

Starting life in a block shape, Chesdale was later manufactured in the foil-wrapped segments packed in a round tray we're so familiar with today. In the last decade an alternative has been the individually wrapped Chesdale slices for easy sandwich-making.

'We are the boys from down on the farm, we really know our cheese
There's much better value in Chesdale, it never fails to please
Chesdale slices thinly, never crumbles, there's no waste
And boy, it's got a mighty taste
Chesdale cheese — it's finest cheddar, made better!'

In the years BIP (Before Instant Puds), it was junket that was put before children for dessert and at birthday parties. And it was only years later that townie kids might have appreciated the awful connection between their sweet dessert and all those bobby calf shelters you saw when driving through the countryside. You might have realised that on dairy farms, which were in the business of getting milk from cows, male or bobby calves weren't a lot of use. But what wasn't clear was their eventual fate and their contribution to New Zealand's cheese industry. The production of cheeses requires the activation of a curdling agent and the most efficient is the rennin enzyme — most commonly known as rennet — which is obtained from the fourth stomach of a milkfed bobby calf.

The main supplier of rennet to the cheese industry in this country has been the New Zealand Co-op Rennet Company, formed in 1916 to meet the demand for cheese rennet, imports of which had been upset by the First World War. Within a few years a rennet extraction operation had been established here and this in turn led to the beginnings of the bobby calf industry.

In the mid 1920s NZ Co-op Rennet Co diversified into home desserts with the introduction of the first instant pudding in the form of Renco, a liquid rennet, for junket. Then, in 1936, came Birthday Renco — coloured versions of Renco in six different fruit flavours. The late 1950s/early 1960s saw junket give way to rennet-free 'quick' instant puddings. Today Renco's main market is in home cheesemaking, while junket itself lingers on only on the menus of some hospitals.

One thing that hasn't changed much in the last 30 years or so is the range of 'penny-sweets' available to Kiwi children. Classics like milk bottles, spearmint leaves, Eskimos, jellybabies, pineapple chunks, jelly aeroplanes, raspberries and blackberries are still available today. From time to time you might even come across a supply of sherberts, the sherbert powder sucked out of its paper envelope through a licorice straw.

In the early '60s things like winegums were eight for a penny (so that even the ha'penny had some use). While the price is higher today, at least in this age where everything else is pre-packed, youngsters can still order sweets singly out of the bulk containers displayed in the fronts of dairy counters.

Whittaker's famous Peanut Slab has evolved from the 5 lb slabs of chocolate that were common before the advent of automatic moulding machines. These hand-moulded slabs were produced with impressions where the shopkeeper could break off a piece or bar and weigh it before sale. J. H. Whittaker and Sons was established in 1896 originally as a distributor of imported chocolate and confectionery, but later turned to manufacturing these items themselves. Their Peanut Slab today sells many millions of bars each year in both New Zealand and Australia. Popular too are the same company's 'K' bars.

From Karitane to kaput

Try as they might the new bloods on the takeaway scene, Kentucky Fried Chicken, McDonalds, Pizza Hut and their ilk, cannot unseat dear old fish and chips as New Zealand's most popular takeaway meal. A recent national survey put the local greasy as the source of nearly 50 percent of all such meals, way ahead of second placegetter, Chinese food, at 21 percent and four times as popular as KFC and McDonalds at about 12 percent each. While it's true that fish and chipperies have a greater spread than franchise outlets to date, in marketing jargon this result rates the New Zealand market as 'unevolved' in terms of the market share held by the fast-food biggies. It also probably partly reflects that side of the New Zealand character that reacts against certain kinds of consumer persuasion and in this case would rather be dead than fed too completely on the American brand.

In the days before the zipper had become commonplace on trousers and boys' shorts, buttons were used to close trouser 'flys'. It was not the most secure of closing systems and the readiness with which fly buttons could part company from buttonholes without warning was a little disconcerting. At school at least there was always someone only too happy to let you know when this had occurred, with cries of 'Your medals are showing' or 'It's one o'clock at the waterworks' (or two, or three etc.)

'**P**rice of wool's gone down!', some joker would say as you returned newly shorn from the barber, the fine prickly stubble at the back and sides of your head contrasting with the Brylcreamed longer top hair. Before the influence of the Liverpool Mop-Tops, the uniform coiffure for the Kiwi male, both young and old, was the no-nonsense short-back-and-sides. What began as an army requirement during the First World War became in the years following a universal Anzac fashion until the early 1960s.

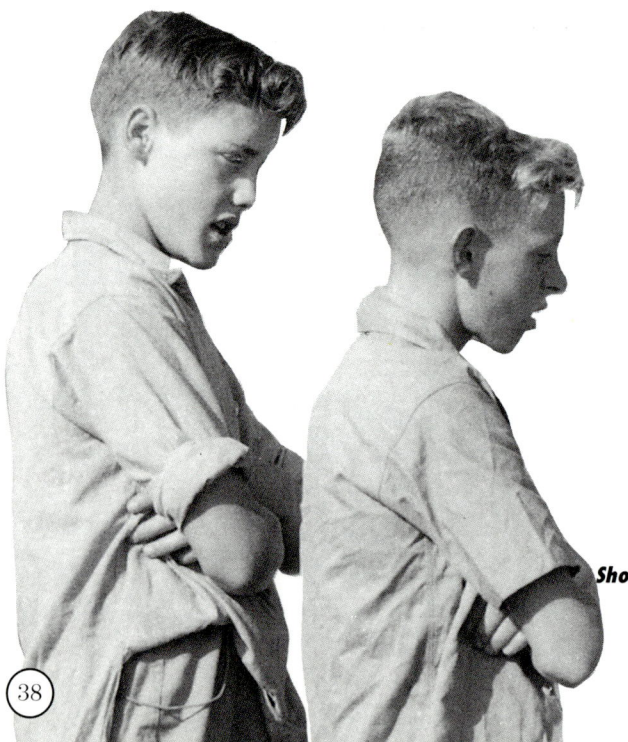

Short-back-and-sides, fifties-style

In the days before television took hold, going to the flicks on a Saturday afternoon — the 1.30 matinée — was a weekend treat. Every town and most city suburbs sported a picture theatre, a 'local' that you could get to easily on foot or by bicycle. And it wasn't expensive. In the early sixties; 9d would get you a seat, 1s 3d a better one. It didn't matter much what was on or that among the shorts might be part six of some adventure serial of which you hadn't seen any of the previous parts. A lot of your schoolmates were there and it was as much a social get-together as cinematic experience. Particularly following the interval when, laden with ice-creams and sweets, the now armed and potentially dangerous audience might occasionally let loose — perhaps with ice-creams dropped scoop-down from front circle seats on the heads of hapless stallees beneath. Traditional was the rolling of Jaffas from the back rows down along the inclined wooden floors. And in those less strictly controlled theatres the simmering excitement could sometimes explode with a barrage of Jaffas fired at the screen, sufficiently forceful at times to knock back the screen and cause the film to go momentarily out of focus.

Television is of course responsible for much of the rot that has affected cultural identity. First transmitted in Auckland in 1960 it was a novelty that New Zealanders were at first wary of, although weekend evenings in particular would see those households with television playing host to crowds of less fortunate friends and neighbours keen to sit and stare in awe at the flickering screen. Before many years had passed, however, most of us were at it, crowding around for *Bonanza*, its credits played over a burning map of the Ponderosa, and paying attention when the radiating-signal-from-transmission-mast graphic accounced the news each evening, to the accompaniment of a voice-over intoning 'North...East...West...South — the News!' Life really hasn't been the same since.

From Karitane to kaput

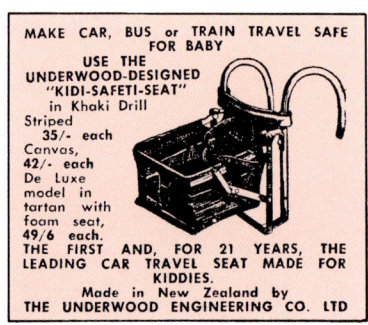

Jack Underwood, Fun Ho!'s originator, was an inveterate inventor who, in addition to toys, turned his attention to baby products. During the 1930s, concerned about the safety of small children in cars, he designed and made the classic Kiddie Safety Seat, a canvas clip-on seat that continued to be used through to the 1960s.

The famous Fun Ho! trademark was designed in 1939 by E. Mervyn Taylor (1906-1964), a New Zealand artist, typographer and designer whose work did much to create an awareness of good design.

*F*un Ho! toys were to New Zealand children of the two postwar decades what Matchbox toys were to British children of the same era. Rudimentary in construction but rugged with it, Fun Ho! were our very own sandpit toys. Their origins go back to the mid-1930s when H. J. (Jack) Underwood, a Wellington civil servant, began turning out moulded lead toys in the basement of his home as a hobby. But a few years later he decided to quit his job and go into toymaking full-time, using Fun Ho! as his brand name.

About 1940 Jack Underwood set up a small non-ferrous foundry to make special metal componentry for firms engaged on war production. Between contracts he continued to make his lead toys and, in addition, the first of the

company's cast-aluminium toys. These early models were mostly copies of American and British cast-iron toys belonging to the Underwood children. They met with an enthusiastic reception on the local toy market.

Throughout the forties, the scarcity of imported toys — at first because of wartime shortages and later because of import control restrictions — meant that Fun Ho! toys enjoyed an almost captive market. As the business expanded and other products in addition to toys were made, the need for more space saw the company move first to New Plymouth and then in 1948 to Inglewood.

At this time the various divisions of the company were brought together under the umbrella of The Underwood

Engineering Company Ltd, later more commonly known as 'Underwood of Inglewood'. In 1963 the company introduced a new series of zinc die-cast toys known as Fun Ho! Midgets. They initially appeared chromed and coppered but were later painted.

Underwoods expanded its activities into cast aluminium and tube furniture and in 1979, after purchasing much of the Auckland based Tri-ang Pedigree operation, plastic ride-ons, tricycles, bicycles and pedal cars began to be manufactured at the factory in Inglewood. Over this entire period of time the cast aluminium Fun Ho! toys were growing in range as well as quantity and by then the name Fun Ho! had become a household word synonymous with long-lasting wheeled toys.

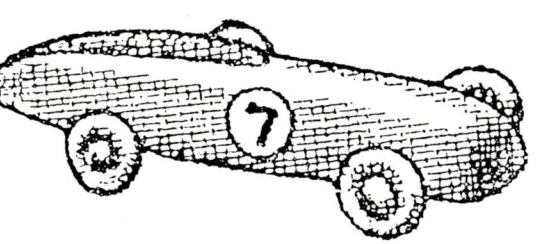

Model No. 76, a small racing car, was the first of the Fun Ho! sand-cast toys. The original wheels for the small Fun Ho! toys were simply rounds hand-punched from quarter-inch sheet rubber. About 1952 cast-plastic wheels replaced them. No. 76 led a series of Fun Ho! racing cars.

The illustration here was one of a number drawn for use in press advertisements. While the toys were never intended as collectors' items — they were made and marketed as durable, long-lasting knock-about toys — their unrefined appearance added charm, and today they are sought out by a growing number of enthusiasts.

The 1970s saw sweeping changes in import licencing regulations, opening the way to a veritable flood of cheap plastic toys. Sales of the Fun Ho! toys plummeted and by the 1980s only a very small range of the cast toys was being manufactured, in ever decreasing quantities.

Fun Ho! aluminium toys are cast in sand, a simple time-worn process nonetheless well suited to the economics of the New Zealand market. Barry Young, for many years the company's purchasing officer, describes here just how the toys are made:

'A pair of steel moulding boxes are used that have sides only but no tops or bottoms. A double-sided plate with the shape of the toy to be moulded is sandwiched between the two moulding boxes, which are then placed flat on the floor of the foundry, or on low benches.

'A specially fine sand, almost like clay, which comes from Dunedin, is shovelled into the uppermost box, the sandwiched plate forming the bottom. The sand is then rammed tight and compacted. Next, the two boxes together with the sandwiched plate are turned upside down on the floor or bench, carefully, so as not to disturb the compacted sand in the first box. Sand is then compacted into the second box. Carefully this box of sand is then lifted clear of the plate, the sand remaining undisturbed in the box with the impression of the plate on the surface.

'Next the plate in the second box is gently removed, leaving its imprint on the sand also. The first box of sand is then replaced on top of the other. You now have two moulding boxes, each tightly packed with sand, fitted together as one, with a cavity in the sand equal to the displacement formed by the two sides of the plate.

'A hole about 35 mm diameter is carefully made through the sand to the cavity into which molten aluminium is poured to form the actual casting. After about 10 to 20 minutes of cooling time, the casting is ''broken out'' of the sand in the moulding boxes and the cast toy is ready for ''fettling''. This involves a series of procedures such as sawing the pouring stem off and filing away any sharp edges or deformities.

'The fettled and cleaned toy now has the axle-holes drilled in place and is ready for painting.'

From Karitane to kaput

*T*he inspired creation of Auckland brothers Hector (Hec) and John Ramsey, the Buzzy Bee has endeared itself to millions of New Zealanders. An intriguing concoction of clackety-clack sound, quivering antennae, spinning wings and bold colour, this delightful pull-along toy has been produced in the hundreds of thousands since its first release in the mid 1940s.

From turning out wooden cores for toilet rolls and wooden doorknobs, Hec Ramsey first ventured into toys with the release of the famous Mary Lou doll in 1941. It was an immediate hit — with generations of New Zealanders destined to cut their first teeth on its beaded limbs — and soon after other character wooden toys were added, including Richard Rabbit, Oscar Ostrich and Dorable Duck.

John Ramsey joined the company after demobbing at the end of the war and was instrumental in designing the Buzzy Bee and sourcing the tawa from which it was made.

The postwar 'baby boom' and import restrictions saw yearly sales of Buzzy Bee in its heyday of the early fifties hit 40,000. Following a fire at the New Lynn factory in the late 1970s, the Buzzy Bee operation was sold into a number of different hands before its purchase by K. T. Lawson Group, its current owners. While the original cardboard wings — which tended to suffer at the teeth of young children — have been swapped for plastic ones, Buzzy Bee in middle age is little altered. And it is poised for a new, international release.

Exterior and interior views of the H. E. Ramsey factory, New Lynn, 1950s.

Only ever made for the local market before, Buzzy Bee exports are planned to the United States and Britain. But our native forests at least are safe: Buzzy Bee is now manufactured in a small town near Shanghai, along with many other toys from the original Ramsey range.

Kris Kricket.

Peter Pup.

Playful Puss.

From Karitane to kaput

Tip Top delivery trucks, late 1930s.

New Zealanders are high achievers in a number of areas — the consumption of beer in particular. But our world rankings improve to third place when it comes to ice cream. By managing 18 litres per person per annum we have also firmly established another reputation, that of Tip Top.

Today's ice-cream giant had classic humble beginnings, in this case the Royal ice cream factory in Dunedin. In the early 1930s the then manager, Len Malaghan, and one of his customers, a shop–owner in the Octagon, decided to go it alone. Malaghan, by the way of American contacts, had evolved an ice cream recipe of his own and in 1935 he and his new partner, Bert Hayman, left for Wellington and immediately leased premises on Manners Street. Here they

opened a new type of shop selling solely ice creams and milk shakes — New Zealand's very first milkbar.

The etymological origins of 'Tip Top' are attributed to a chance overheard remark. In search of a name, and a meal, Malaghan and Hayman were seated in a restaurant when they heard a fellow diner use the term in praise of the service. The expression 'tip top' was then part of the vernacular and widely exploited commercially — hardly surprising in such a mountainous country. An early use was by Turner and Turner of Wellington on their alliterative Tip Top teas in 1903, labouring the 'point' with images of peaks as well. Then in 1917 other tea merchants in Taihape had the Three 'T's Ceylon blend, representing 'That Tip-Top Taste'. In 1930

the Wairarapa Farmers' Co-operative of Masterton began employing a toy spinning-top trademark on Tip Top iodised calf meal. Also decisively beating the ice cream to the name was Tip Top furniture and linoleum polish, by Rolfe and Co. of Auckland, in 1931.

But by the end of the thirties Tip Top milkbars were nearly as well known, having spread from Wellington to the lower half of the North Island, Nelson and Blenheim.

Ice cream manufacturers in New Zealand have gone the same way as our breweries and cordial factories but in the period from the early 1940s through the 1950s the country could lay claim to over a hundred ice-cream companies. The period also charted the rise and fall of another national institution — the

The country's first ice cream was hand-churned and sold from handcarts. Later, when milkbars began to proliferate, much of the early ice cream manufacturing took place on those premises. The ice cream was sold over the counter and, if it had a brand name at all, it took the name of the milkbar.

When ice cream making became more business-like and was removed to separate factories, many of the original brand names were carried over, so that by the late 1940s a list of the country's ice cream makers included such evocative names as:

Havmor (Nelson)
Top Notch (Christchurch)
Everest (Christchurch)
Perfection (Christchurch)
Sunshine (Nelson)
Lucky (Westport)
Westland Snowflake (Greymouth)
Blue Bell (Greymouth)
Arctic (Wellington)

Tip Top (Wellington)
Glacier (Palmerston North)
Aurora (New Plymouth)
Egmont (New Plymouth)
Delecta (New Plymouth)
Peter Pan (Waipukurau)
Blue Moon (Hastings)
Ruapehu (Taumarunui)
Rosco (Hamilton)
Alpine (Huntly)

The Kiwi Milk Bar, Wellington, late 1950s.

milkbar. In Dunedin in 1942, for example, there were, in addition to the Tip Top bars located at 1 and 104 Princes Street, the Bungalow, Delecta, Elige, O.K. and the inevitable Adelphi and Strand. In Invercargill, milkbars in the '40s were more quaint than cosmopolitan: the Blue Bird, Brown Owl and Peter Pan. Balclutha, it seems, had more patriotic milkbars, with the Kiwi and Southern Cross. And in Roxburgh one was presumably drawn to the Magnet for ice creams and milk shakes. Furthest south, even Bluff had two — Denton's and Doyle's — both on Gore Street.

Theoretically, the northern climate makes ice cream more of a year-round habit. In 1928 Auckland had three producers: the Astrella, New Polar and Robinson's. At Gisborne there was the Friesia, presumably honouring the cows that made it all possible, and in 1936 Palmerston North had two factories, the Cherry Blossom and E-Tan.

When Tip Top arrived in Auckland in 1938, the new company was pitted against six others. These included McDonald's — makers of the Duchess ice-cream block — and the resilient Robinson's. There was also Peters of Newmarket, who had a double-handled 'Two-in-One' ice cream and chocolate treat on a stick, and the Oasis Ice Cream Factory of Cook Street. The last would have been related to the Oasis Milkbars, conveniently spaced at 65, 265 and 282 Queen Street.

In addition to standard cones these establishments had their own registered Choc Bloks, forerunners of the modern Topsy. The competitive nature of the novelty business was expressed by W. J. Carbines of Mt Eden in 1939. His chocolate-coated Boms had a truly military flavour. By then Tip Top was well dug in, with supply depots at 53a and 242 Queen Street as well as 211 Broadway, Newmarket. Alternative Auckland rendezvous included the Apex, Metropole, Milady, Roxy, Treasure, Snack and Tumble Inn. Over the harbour at Devonport were three more: one Tip Top as well as the Shelma and Serville.

During the war years the thousands of American servicemen who came here on R & R brought with them a huge passion for ice cream and an influence on milkbar decor and menu that would last into the 1950s.

As opposed to the traditional tea-

From Karitane to kaput

Ice cream novelties have always been one of Tip Top's strong suits. They frequently reflect events or fads, but on one or two occasions have resulted in something really unusual if not bizarre. Such a category must include the red, white and blue scoop ice cream produced for the 1963 Royal Tour, and another, called 'Black Gold', of the same decade. Produced to commemorate an All Black tour, Black Gold by all accounts combined a hideous black colour with a licorice flavour. Fortunately it seems to have lingered less in the memory than it must have done in the mouth. More fondly recalled is the alliterative and now deceased TT2, the classic ice-block of the fifties and sixties and a mainstay

of summer holidays for New Zealand children. While its name was no more meaningful than the American borrowing of 'popsicle' that has replaced it, it was ours.

room, the modern milkbars were obviously aimed at the youthful end of the market. Weaned on the new fizzy drinks and sodas this generation would shortly be introduced to another American import and milkbar stock-in-trade, Coca-Cola. By the '50s, however, the coffee bar was coming into its own, and things European were *en vogue*. And just as milkbars and coffee bars became indistinguishable at times, so their names drew from a mix of American, Continental and, to a lesser extent, Caribbean influences. Thus Wellington had the Brooklyn, Californian Coffee Shop, Virginian and Waldorf. Suggestive of Europe were the Casa Fontana, Corinthia, Florence, La Fiesta, La Scala and Sorrento.

Manufacturing Wellington's ice cream

in the '50s were the Supercold and Arctic factories. But best remembered is Frosty Jack, personified by the jolly anoraked Eskimo with the Bill Haley quiff who graced the Eskimo Pie, a product dating from the mid '20s. Jack himself had first appeared in the late '40s, working for Frozen Products of Tennyson Street.

The early '60s saw the passing of an era. Of milkbars and coffee bars Auckland alone hosted a staggering 240, with the latter very much in ascendance. The Expresso, Coffee Pot, Coffee Time and Cona Coffee Bar were obviously not pushing milk shakes or ice creams. The Fiesta, Brazil and Rio were also celebrating the caffeine revival, but perhaps the New American and Yankee milkbars still maintained links with the

old tradition. Many milkbars, of course, did not disappear in the face of new competition. They simply carried on, in the corner of the dairy or grocery store where they'd always been.

The 1950s were the halcyon days of the fourpenny (4d) ice-cream, available in such flavours as basic plain, vanilla and hokey pokey. Just as popular was the ice-block on a stick, the rather watery (by today's standards) TT2. Apparently there was no TT1. Consumers soon learned the inflation technique to unstick the wrapper from the frozen lolly.

By 1951 Tip Top factories in Auckland and Wellington were producing the equivalent of 55 million ice creams per year. In addition to cones these included cartons and 'dixies' — tubs with

Peculiar to New Zealand is its famous hokey-pokey ice cream, a blend of vanilla base with pieces of toffee. Made famous by Tip Top, it was first sold in this country by the Meadowgold Ice Cream Company of Papatoetoe, Auckland, in the 1940s.

The idea of adding toffee to ice cream wasn't new — in the United States so called 'candy' flavours were common and to this day there are similar ice creams such as 'Butter Brickle' — but what was unique was the distinctive taste imparted by hokey-pokey toffee. The first hokey-pokey recipe, similar to the one made familiar by the *Edmonds Cookbook*, involved caramelising sugar and adding soda. The resultant aeration produced, when the mixture set, the familiar honeycomb structure. Unfortunately it also gradually broke down and melted inside the ice cream, leaving a syrupy puddle. The recipe was therefore altered to produce toffee that would retain its crunch.

For many years after Tip Top introduced the flavour in the early 1950s the toffee was formed in large sheets and then broken up with hammers for distribution into the vanilla base. Irregular sized and shaped pieces of toffee caused occasional jamming of the feeding unit and recently — with the greater need for reliability required by modern high-volume machines — Tip Top has changed to standardised, pelletised hokey-pokey. It tastes the same as ever but one can still regret the passing of the sharp-edged nuggets of toffee.

Hokey Pokey

5 tbsp sugar
2 tbsp golden syrup
1 tsp bicarbonate soda

Bring sugar and golden syrup to the boil, slowly stirring all the time. Boil 4 minutes, stirring occasionally. Remove from heat and add bicarbonate soda. Stir in quickly until it froths and pour at once into a greased tin. Break up when cold. Store in air-tight jars.

lift-up tops and small wooden spoons enclosed. Also, there was a coated frozen novelty called Tip Toppa and the Kapai block. Probably the most recent in a line of products — including boots and brooms — capitalising on the Maori word for 'it's good', this Kapai was an ice-cream block sandwiched between pink wafers.

About 1960 the Auckland factory changed its name to General Foods, only to revert back in 1988. For years the Auckland and Wellington operations had been independent, each agreeing to keep within a line connecting the northernmost points of Tongaporutu, Pipiriki, Waiouru, Tarawera and Hick's Bay. When the two companies finally merged in 1960, General Foods assumed a national coverage and 55 percent of the country's ice cream output. Then in 1963 the company took over the Supreme factory which had been operating in Timaru since the '30s. Another addition to the stable was Walls in 1979, previously part of Unilever.

While Tip Top has steadily overwhelmed its traditional opposition, new names have popped up. In the early '60s there was the aggressively promoted American-style (and proud of it) Rosco brand. Today Tip Top's main competition has similar inspirations — New American, made by United Dairy Foods. To meet the challenge, both manufacturers — and a few others beside — now increasingly stress the natural qualities and superior taste and texture of their products.

When Tip Top was born, few homes could claim electric refrigeration, and ice-chests and meat safes were poor substitutes. Butter, cream and jellies, for example, could only be kept cool in porous containers which required regular soaking in cold water. Also available in sizes costing from 3/6 upwards, was the 1937 Iceberg ice-chest, with a plate-glass bottom and needing 'no ice'. Equally cheap to keep was the 'Xtracool', an up-market meat safe maintained with 'a little water twice weekly'. But by 1935 the electric refrigerator had begun to appear, and its benefits were being stressed: 'Completely eliminates the otherwise ever-present danger of food contamination by flies, dust and atmospheric impurities'. Thus, names like Servel, Crosley Shelvador, Gilfillan and Froskist entered the homes of New

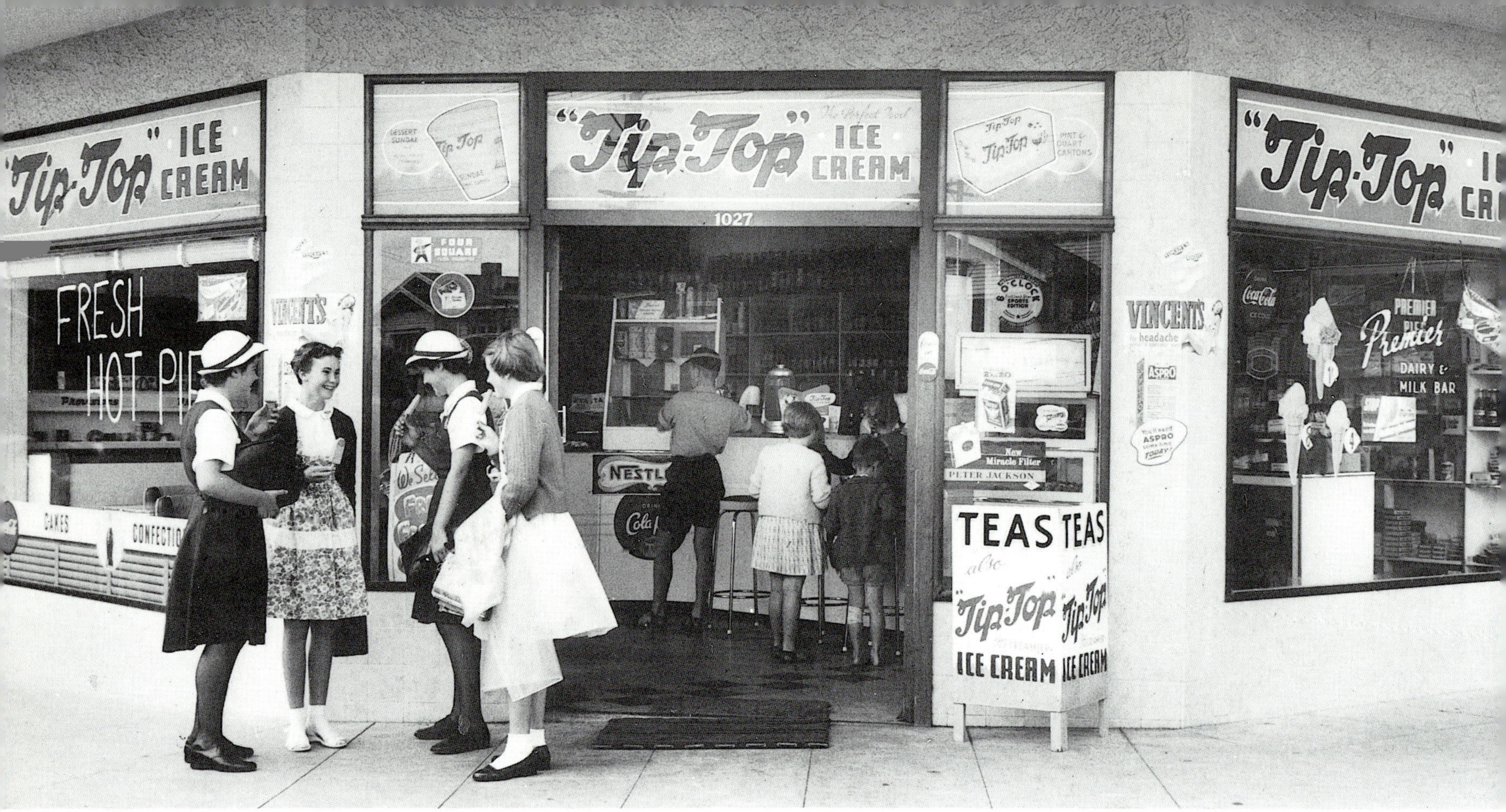

The Premier Dairy and Milk Bar, Great North Road, Auckland, early 1960s.

Zealanders. For many folk, ice cream had until then been a summer treat, available only from the milkbar or dairy. Eventually, with the take-home pack and a 'fridge', it also became a regular dessert.

By 1988 Tip Top had 60 percent of the market, three times the share of its nearest rival, New American. But licking the opposition means the constant cranking out of new season's models and novelties. Since the rather bland TT2 days there has been a regular supply of these, including Choc Bar, Fru-Ju, Moggy Man, Toppa and Topsy. Some only last the season, but others return, up-dated. The 1988 model of the Trumpet, for example, had the inside of the cone double-sprayed with chocolate to maintain its crunchiness. For inspiration the Tip Top design team looks to where many of their customers look — television and the movies. Thus the *Thunderbirds* series and Disney's *Mary Poppins* have both been immortalised in confectionery.

Nevertheless, there are problems for the ice-cream industry in New Zealand, with the population not so much growing as just getting older. The manufacturers therefore need to ensure continued adult awareness of their products. While the more sophisticated Tandem and Movenpick are intended to re-awaken mature audiences to ice-cream possibilities, the promotion of ice cream generally will continue to recall the endless summers of one's childhood and the cone ice creams that went with them.

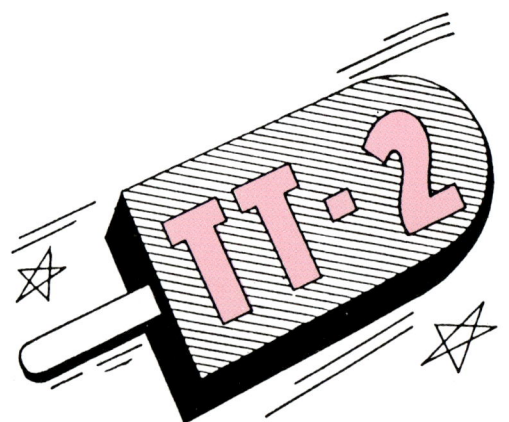

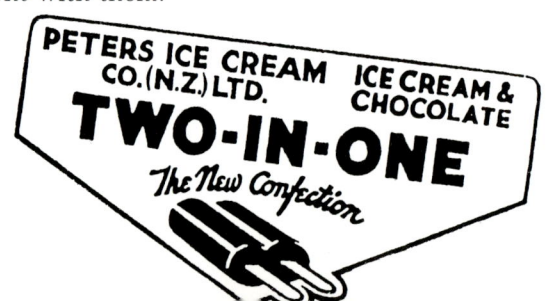

Barefoot to school.

*G*oing barefoot has long been part of the New Zealand way of life — from the earliest Polynesian colonisers onwards. But New Zealand has also developed distinctive footwear styles of its own.

In 1886 there were 31 boot factories in this country, making the industry one of our major employers. With 1299 hands it ranked only behind sawmills and printing works, and just headed off gold-mining. One hundred and forty of these footwear workers were with R. Hannah & Co. of Wellington, still a big name in boots today. Back in the 1880s the company was producing some 100,000 pairs of boots and shoes per year, ranging from the everyday hobnailed watertight variety for West Coast miners, to the 'gentlemen's porpoise-hide shooting boot'.

No doubt the New Zealand terrain ensured a steady market for the former but it was not just miners who needed boots. Boys and girls also wore them, over thick woollen stockings. Their parents were of the opinion that young ankles needed to be firmly supported in stout footwear.

Hannah's has survived but many other popular boot brands have fallen by the wayside. At the turn of the century Auckland's Kapai Boot Factory claimed to be the North Island's largest, producing 6000 pairs per month. Elsewhere in Auckland the Northern Boot and Shoe Manufacturing Co. was assembling the more uplifting Aurora and Northern Light brands. From down south in Dunedin came Sargood, Son and Ewen's functional Standard boot,

introduced about 1875. Meanwhile, Christchurch was the home town of the loyal Zealandia, made by Skelton, Frostick and Co. since the 1880s and still around in the mid 1920s. Another old firm was O'Brien & Co. whose O'B boots have protected toilers in factories and on football fields from as early as 1866.

From stout beginnings New Zealand's footwear has loosened considerably. Informality is now the keynote. While Victorians and Edwardians buckled and laced up for protection, later generations have adopted an increasingly casual approach. Early children's sandals did — to a minor extent — let the sun shine in, but were a far cry from the footwear of today. Popular for several generations has been the perennial, leather Roman sandal — standard summer issue for both

From Karitane to kaput

Characteristic of growing up in the antipodes is the summertime proliferation of young feet sporting bloodied tops to their big toes — the end result of bare feet plus speed plus a concrete or asphalt path. Classically, the toe is stubbed hard enough to remove a large flap of skin from the top of the toe, the flap remaining hinged at the back while blood gushes freely from the gouged flesh. At school, once the initial pain had passed, it was a case of hobbling to the school nurse or some teacher for mecurochrome and perhaps a gauze bandage. These modern days of sneaker-and-jandal-shod feet have probably seen a decline in the frequency of the condition.

primary and secondary schools. In addition to compulsory use this basic sandal almost gained fashion status in the 1970s. Like blue jeans the sandal improved with age, being worn until the straps parted or soles delaminated. The history of New Zealand casual footwear is best illustrated by two colourful success stories — the plastic sandal and the jandal. Both ideas were imported from overseas, but were soon adopted as our own.

At the end of the Second World War, two resourceful New Zealand soldiers in Britain saw potential in plastic strip being manufactured there. The soldiers, Mick Kyne and Mervyn Devine, imported a quantity of this novel material to New Zealand and began converting it into watch straps and then belts. The pair

also formed their own company in about 1956 to handle the distribution of various shoes marketed under the Kaydee Footwear label, the name inspired by their own surnames. When a French 'sandale plastique' brought to New Zealand by an airline pilot came to the attention of Plastic Products of Hamilton, this company approached Kyne and Devine to market a local version, and so our first plastic sandal, the Kaydee, was born.

Subsequent growth of the market for plastic sandals was not without problems. When the first sample was shown to the buyer for Hannah's he was so impressed by the agent's enthusiasm that he ordered large quantities in every size. Unfortunately, because of high initial costs, Kaydee were only able to

supply them in size 11. However, consumer reaction was positive enough to allow the range to be increased by three or four sizes each season. This was despite considerable resistance in some quarters to the idea of plastic footwear, a prejudice fuelled by concerns for health and status. Some mothers would not put their children in Kaydees on principle, regarding them simply as a poor man's sandal. There were further problems at school where they tended to skid on shiny classroom floors, and small stones lodged in the soles only made things worse.

In some cases 'cheap' did mean 'nasty' as Kaydees were to discover. Some of the competitors' shoes fell apart so reliably that the whole plastic footwear business got a bad name,

eventually convincing Mervyn Devine to sell his company to Bing Harris.

Plastic sandals have steadily slipped in popularity, but at their peak Kaydees could sell a quarter of a million pairs per year in New Zealand. Curiously the New Zealand market only ever existed in the area north of Taupo, but the sandals enjoyed some major overseas markets as well. Papua New Guinea and Fiji were once major markets, now lost to far cheaper Taiwanese imports.

The only other components of the plastic sandals were the equally durable nickel-plated rivets and buckles, which have always been supplied by a firm in Melbourne. It was in Australia that Kaydees sold best — one million pairs in their most successful year. A further achievement in that country was the

adoption of Kaydees over traditional leather sandals by the Australian Navy.

The late 1950s saw the birth in New Zealand of another type of casual footwear — simpler even than Kaydees. In 1957 a New Zealand sales represent- ative named Maurice Yock, who worked in his grandfather's company J. Yock & Co., was travelling through Asia when he was inspired by local footwear to introduce to this country that item of footwear known elsewhere as flip-flops and thongs. With a name unique to New Zealand and derived from 'Japanese sandal', the jandal went into production in a Te Papapa garage. The business was simply called Jandals Ltd.

At first the rubber sheets from which the jandals were punched out came from Hong Kong, but with

importation problems Skellerup took over the supply of raw materials and eventually bought the jandal side of the business altogether.

'Jandal' is a registered trademark but like many other brand names has now passed into common usage, describing a type of footwear in general. Bata produced their own version, as did Feltex with 'Polynesian Thongs'. Much less scrupulous was one manufacturer, believed to be from Taranaki, who supplied garages with a cheaper variant advertised as Jandels.

The official jandal spent the first two years of its life being brown and white. Plain colours and candy-stripes followed, but it is blue that has proved the most popular colour.

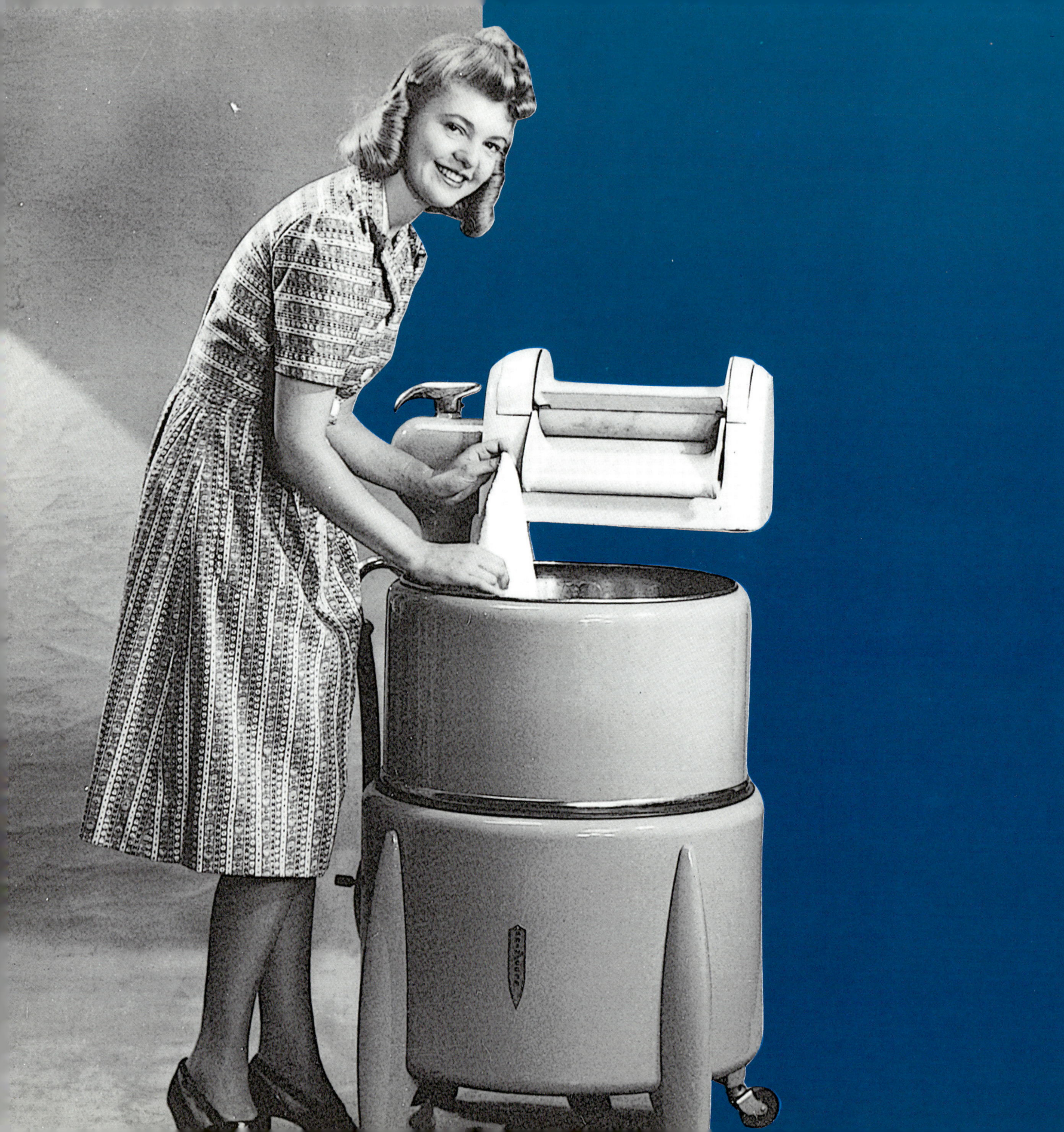

Home

and Hosed

Home and hosed

Diggers' hut, Westport.

Maori meeting house with thatched roof and walls.

*T*he first European shelters in this country were not unlike the early Maori whare — hardly surprising in view of the available resources. But whereas Europeans have traditionally catered for all domestic functions under the one roof (except in the case of early toilets and washhouses, when existing technology made this impossible) the Maori house had but one room and one activity. Different houses were therefore required for sleeping, cooking, storing food and communal meeting. At first they were simply lean-to shelters with roofs of flax leaves to keep out the cold. An improved version with a sunken floor to give more headroom appears to be a local development, with no Polynesian precedent. These were thatched with toe-toe and rushes, as were the covers

for the storage pits of the precious kumara. Eventually, more generous houses with vertical walls allowed the occupants to stand up. In Polynesia such structures were thatched with split coconut or pandanus leaves, but in Aotearoa home-builders used the southernmost palm, the nikau.

The popular idea of Maori architecture is not the modest dwelling described above, but rather the whare whakairo, the carved meeting house. The richly decorated maihi (bargeboards) and vertical amo framing the porch constitute an enduring image of Maori culture. Although dating only from the mid 19th century, these structures — 20 metres and over in length — also represent one of the highest achievements of Maori art.

If the great carved whare whakairo

reflects elements of European architecture, this would not be the first time the two traditions had colluded. Much earlier, Maori bushcraft had evolved basic shelter techniques which were passed on to the first European visitors and settlers. Later 'whare' entered the everyday vocabulary as a small house or hut, as for example the seasonal shearers' quarters on a back-country sheep farm.

The first European dwellings were often ingenious responses to local conditions and materials. A single-storey raupo cottage, for example, betrayed very little of the English origins of its owners. Unfortunately, they might soon discover that native roofing was neither as waterproof nor as permanent as their familiar English thatch. Because of the

Logging, North Auckland.

uncertainty of early colonial life these houses were temporary and basic — really little more than wooden tents. Soon an abundance of sawn timber provided a more substantial exterior, as had been the practice in the earlier colonies of Australia and America. Inside, rooms were lined with horizontal rough-sawn boards which might receive a cover of wallpaper, plaster or simply the opened-out pages from newspapers and journals of the time. On the roof, totara shingles split badly in the sun so were no great advance on raupo thatch. However, there was corrugated iron, first manufactured in New Zealand in Dunedin in 1869 but imported much earlier. Its preferred use in England for temporary buildings and fencing did not prevent it from becoming part of our culture, and 120 years later,

still our favourite roofing material.

In early 19th-century Britain the popular terrace house was considered an appropriate style to transplant in Australia. But later, across the Tasman, New Zealand missed out on this distinctive architecture. In the intervening years the terrace had somewhat fallen from favour, but more dramatic was the vulnerability of its brick construction to earthquakes. Nevertheless, a few isolated pockets did infiltrate these shores. But probably the major factor in our renunciation of the terrace was the sheer availability of land and timber. Thus began the realistic dream of home-ownership for all. Over the years the once inexhaustible kauri has given way to other natives and imported timbers, and eventually to

treated pine. The archetypal quarter-acre section may have shrunk in order to squeeze everybody in, and a home of one's own is, increasingly, beyond the reach of many, but the standard New Zealand home, itself an icon of our culture, continues to be the free-standing single-storey bungalow — a style which was, like corrugated iron, scorned back home in 19th-century England.

Home and hosed

The villa.

We will never know how many raupo huts and temporary shelters were built by New Zealand's first settlers. Similarly, little evidence remains of the earth, cob and mud brick structures of the early European immigrants. Almost by default it is the ubiquitous Victorian villa which has the honour of being our first mass-built home. In the late 19th century the villa was defined as 'a country or suburban residence of some pretensions to elegance'. Even so, it simply came to mean home to many generations of New Zealanders. In the larger centres, with their expanding suburbs now connected by electric tram, this new style of house went unchallenged from about 1880 until the First World War. In the language of the day (1908) they were 'roomy ...

handsome for the most part, centres of graceful hospitality, for which the ample reception-rooms are specially suited'.

Further, there were 'spacious lawns, gardens, plantations and shrubberies ... about them.' Obviously, not all villas were so lucky, but they did share an almost excessive love of ornament. The nation's kauri was at their service, and balustrades, brackets and corbels, once fashioned from stone, were now freely interpreted in timber. Other distinguishing features such as bay-windows and verandahs provided for infinite variations on the theme, so some sort of individuality was preserved.

The villa has served New Zealand well, to put it mildly. As its original residents moved on — perhaps to maintenance-free retirement in the

newer suburbs — the old house assumed new roles. More often than not it was destined to become a flat for transient out-of-towners. These new tenants had to adjust to double-hung windows that rattled in the wind or, because of broken sash cords, refused to operate at all. It was standard for villas to face the street, regardless of sun. Thus, certain rooms retained a mustiness, compounded by layers of aging carpets and sagging Chesterfields. In damper and south-facing areas the process of deterioration was speeded up. The original piles of totara or puriri (the latter perhaps riddled by the grub of the puriri moth) decayed, causing settling. As a result, doors refused to shut and wallpaper bagged and billowed in the wind. There were smaller forces at work as well,

FRONT ELEVATION FOR NO. 4 COTTAGE.

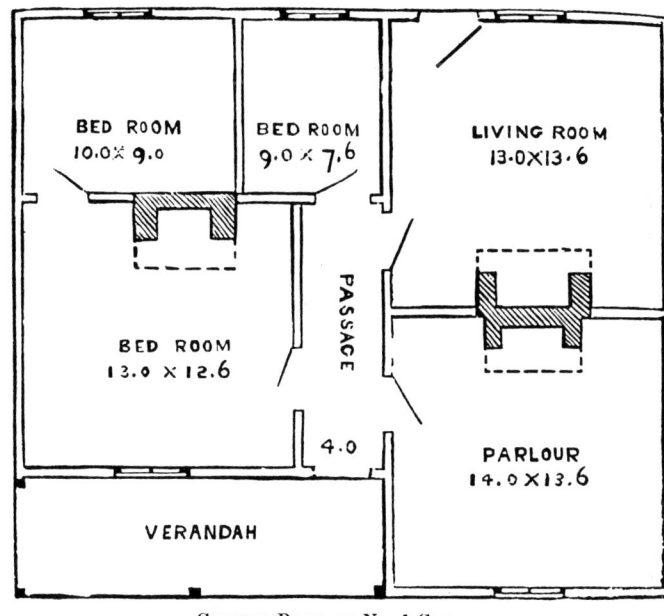

BED ROOM
10.0 × 9.0

BED ROOM
9.0 × 7.6

LIVING ROOM
13.0 × 13.6

PASSAGE

BED ROOM
13.0 × 12.6

PARLOUR
14.0 × 13.6

4.0

VERANDAH

GROUND PLAN OF NO. 4 COTTAGE.

apart from the intrusion of mice with the onset of winter. Voracious boring insects, most noticeably the dreaded two-tooth borer, ate their way along selected sap-filled boards in the tongue and groove flooring.

But for all this, villas can be fondly recalled. For many of the post (Second World) war generation, a villa was the first home away from home and taste of independence. The shabbiness usually associated with flats of this vintage was perhaps in tune with the casual lifestyle of the 1960s. The new surroundings were hardly inhibiting. The extraordinarily high ceilings — made when kauri was plentiful — may have posed heating problems in winter, but assisted air circulation in summer. The central passage doubled as a storeroom for such items as

bicycles and surfboards — vulnerable on the front verandah. The bathroom was usually scarred by ancient plumbing systems such as the fearsome and unpredictable califont. But the original cast-iron bath, resurfaced, on claw feet, could still be in use — served now by plastic pipes. Creative approaches to decorating were also called for to compensate for the villa's complete lack of built-in storage.

On a sloping section the basement might be an uncatalogued museum of ancient appliances and furniture, from cookers to congoleums. Back upstairs, spacious villas were ideal social venues. In addition to 'mixed flatting' — which crept in during the '60s — various rites of passage occurred beneath the board and batten ceilings. People studied,

partied, came of age, lived together (in the de facto sense), split up, got married and even bought villas of their own. Other, freer, spirits may have just crashed for a night or two.

Natural causes alone did not victimise our villas. In the inner gullies of Auckland, for example, motorway development cut an asphalt swath through whole neighbourhoods. Elsewhere, spared this fate, villas were revitalised. The 1970s oil shock had highlighted the advantages of inner-city living, and there was a worldwide return to the metropolis. Thanks to concrete piles and tanalised timber, many of New Zealand's now gentrified villas are in better shape than ever. Their original construction — generous and flexible — allows whole walls to be removed for

Home and hosed

A large number of New Zealanders share their homes with wood-boring insects. Only residents of newer houses, with the benefits of tanalised timber and other modern materials, are spared the ravages of the voracious borer. Villas in particular are familiar with the insects' meandering channels along their floorboards, and the tell-tale piles of fine dust that appear annually under certain pieces of furniture. Despite such damage it is commonly believed that no New Zealand house was ever brought down by borer. However, there is at least one case of demolition necessitated by severe infestation. Many other older houses are said to survive only because their resident borer are holding hands.

The common house borer (Anobium punctatum) specialises in the match-linings of old kitchens and weatherboards on the shady side of the house. Of more concern is the dreaded two-tooth longhorn, a native which supplements its traditional diet of forest timbers with wooden houses. Through its extensive burrowings this insect can reduce timber to a mere shell. In addition, New Zealand termites are also responsible for damage to housing timbers, although it is the Australian species that cause the greatest trouble. These undesirable immigrants have entered the country in imported hardwoods. Some populations have proved so durable that their colonies have survived inside tram

sleepers which have long been asphalted over.

Looking out over any New Zealand town or city reveals a sea of corrugated iron roofs, as has been the case for

generations. The red of iron oxide was almost the only colour for many years, with minor relief provided by green. In the 1920s 'roof paint' was synonymous with red oxide. This was mixed with linseed oil and cost about 13s per gallon. Later, one could opt instead for a 'guaranteed fadeless' permanent green — but at nearly twice the price! A cheap, practical roofing material, corrugated iron also enabled the efficient collection of rainwater off the roof — even if during a really decent downpour the sound of rain on iron made conversation nearly impossible.

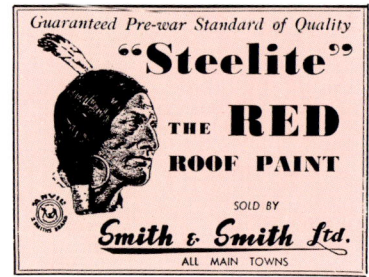

open planning. Villas were always well endowed with chimneys, but many of these have gone, their valuable bricks recycled horizontally as patchwork paving. Original villas ignored the Victorian sun but the modern version embraces it — in conservatories, through French doors and on decks. With new corrugated iron and re-wired, re-plumbed and gibbed, many of these houses will happily accommodate New Zealanders well into the next century.

IVORY WHITE	PEMANENT ROOF GREEN	BRIGHT ROOF RED
LIGHT CREAM	LAVENDER GREY	LIGHT GREY
MIDDLE CREAM	PALE GREEN	CHOCOLATE
DEEP CREAM	SPECIAL VERANDAH GREY	LIGHT STONE

A Hawke's Bay family in the garden of their bungalow house.

The Victorian villa served New Zealand well. It was sturdily constructed, of quality materials, and it faithfully reflected the attitudes of the day. Standing square and central on its section, in rigid rows and infinite permutations, it presented its best face to the street. But about 1910 the ornate facade of the villa began to lose ground to an import from the West Coast of America. After the First World War, New Zealand was ready for a more casual approach to its domestic architecture. This rather homely need found expression in the Californian bungalow, characterised by low-pitched gable roofs, wide eaves, deep porches and heavy exposed beams. Even the villa's troublesome double-hung windows were now obsolete, thanks to side-hinged casements and top-hinged leaded fanlights.

Postwar informality in the home demanded a loosening-up of the floor plan. To begin with, the villa's tunnel-like central passage became truncated, to create an entrance lobby, or vestibule. Everywhere there were now nooks and cosy retreats, complemented by a brilliant new idea: built-in furniture. And whereas the villa had ignored the sun — mainly because its owners wanted to avoid fading the furnishing fabrics — the bungalow was built to enjoy it. The verandah was gone, but health-giving rays could be enjoyed in the comfort of the sun room, made for the job. Other personal matters were also well attended to. The bathroom and lavatory had tentatively entered the villa in the 1890s, at the ends of the passage and back verandah respectively. But the more body-conscious bungalow enthusiastically drew these conveniences into the heart of the house, so that they might be enjoyed in unprecedented luxury.

The age of the bungalow also coincided with other technological advances. Most notably there was electricity, a new alternative to gas, and refrigerators began to edge out the mesh-covered safe. But there were some losses, particularly in the use of kauri, now fast running out. Other native woods were used more — for example, matai in the flooring — and huge quantities of redwood, oregon and cedar from the bungalow's Californian homeland were imported.

The villa had been approached directly, from a central gate, but the

Home and hosed

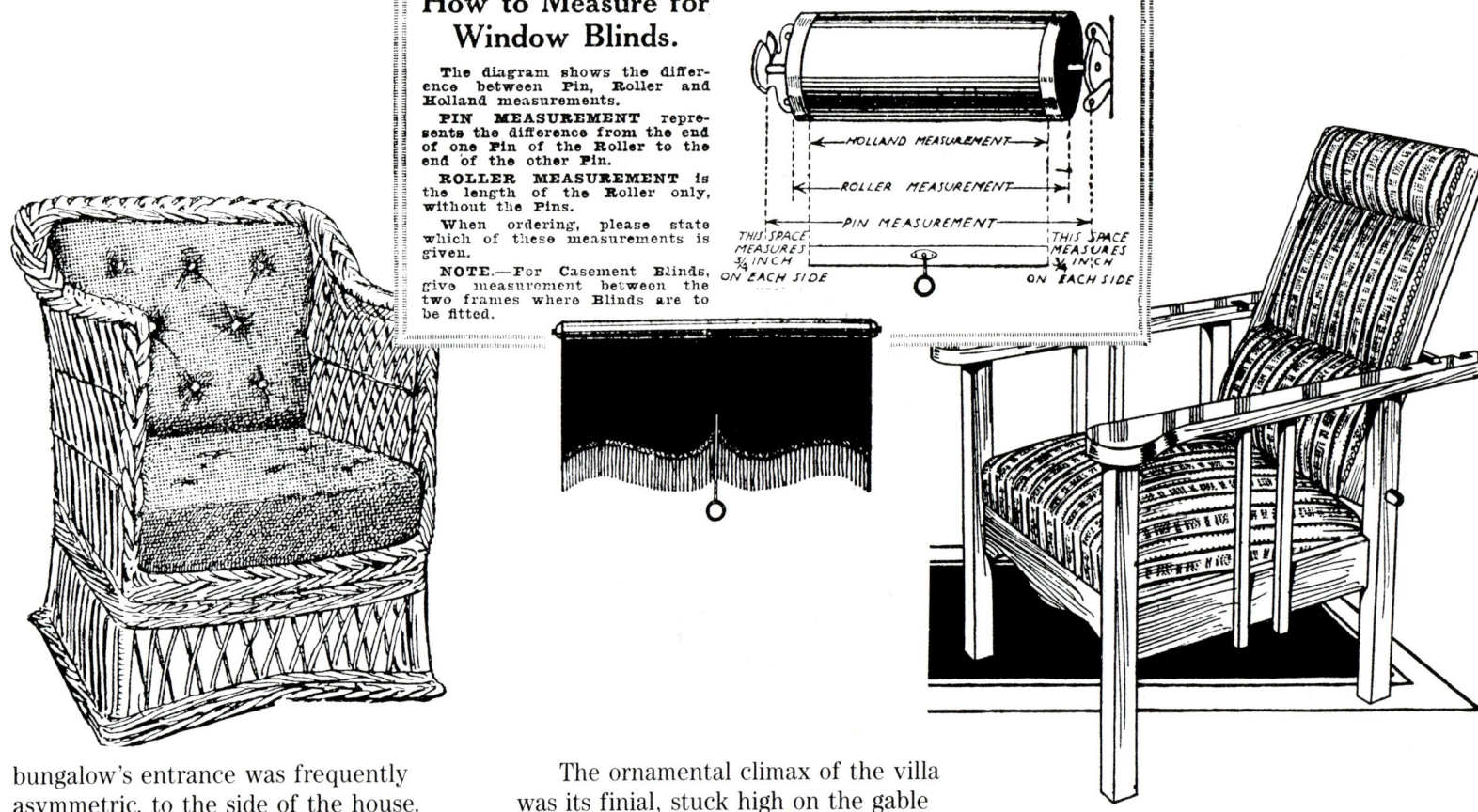

How to Measure for Window Blinds.

The diagram shows the difference between Pin, Roller and Holland measurements.

PIN MEASUREMENT represents the difference from the end of one Pin of the Roller to the end of the other Pin.

ROLLER MEASUREMENT is the length of the Roller only, without the Pins.

When ordering, please state which of these measurements is given.

NOTE.—For Casement Blinds, give measurement between the two frames where Blinds are to be fitted.

bungalow's entrance was frequently asymmetric, to the side of the house. There was also a more major move afoot — the arrival of the carshed, or garage. The bungalow generally had room for this new outhouse on one side of the section, but villas were not so accommodating.

A product familiar to villa renovators and builders alike is gibraltar board, which made its New Zealand debut on the walls of later bungalows. Its smooth plaster finish was both an aesthetic and hygenic improvement on the old wallpaper and scrim system. Above all the gib and the panelling (of figured rimu and oregon) were picture rails, plate racks and dados. A grid ceiling of dark-stained wooden 'beams' may have implied great strength, but also concealed the joins in the lining.

The ornamental climax of the villa was its finial, stuck high on the gable where the bargeboards met. As for colour, this was restricted to a multi-paned window at the end of the verandah. But both of these distinctive features suffered: finials rotted off and weren't replaced and verandahs were converted into extra bedrooms. Bungalows may not have had finials (or even the tall gables to support them) but they did surpass the villa when it came to glass. In better quality residences there might be a decorative window near the entrance porch or the inglenook, and the new fanlights were a boost to the stained glass and leaded-light industries. Certain subjects had been popular for years: floral and rising sun motifs, and the ocean-going galleon in

full sail. Herbert Bros., 'Gold Medal Art Glass Workers' of Bank Street, Auckland, promoted themselves with such a vessel in 1917.

At its most exuberant the bungalow was as distinctive as its neo-Gothic ancestor. But its distinguishing features soon became diluted when, despite the rays of sunshine and galleons on placid oceans, New Zealand entered the Depression of the 1930s. The building industry received a set-back and the bungalow was pared down to a simple rectangular plan with a porch on one side. In better times, Californian culture returned to our shores in other guises, but never again as such an architectural influence.

State house, mid 1930s.

Although statistically one of the world's best-housed nations, New Zealand has always had accommodation problems. Acute shortages during the 1930-35 Depression finally stimulated government action, with distinctive results. New suburbs of state housing sprang up.

The original planning aimed for every house to have its own plot of ground, and a careful spread of a large number of different house-styles to create a harmony of design. John A. Lee, Under-Secretary for Housing in the new Labour Government, made the State's involvement in putting roofs over heads a personal mission. Within a few months of a new Housing Department being set up in 1936, large areas of land had been set aside — in Auckland and Wellington

— and the first houses were completed in the following year. The emphasis was on high standards of construction and convenience, and designs which emphasised things such as kitchens positoned to receive the morning sun. At first all houses were rental, but from 1949 changes in government policy saw tenants being encouraged to buy their houses. Incentive to do so was provided by a family-benefit capitalisation scheme first introduced in 1959. This allowed tenants with families to capitalise their weekly family benefit to a maximum of £1000 for each child, for use in purchasing the unit.

The first state houses showed almost classical proportions in their designs and were either weatherboarded or faced with brick. Roofs were tiled. A radical

departure from the bungalow fashion of the 1920s, the state houses of the 1930s have improved with age. Today they express a soundness of design and construction that is superior to much of the housing built in the 1950s and '60s.

Other government departments have also given the New Zealand landscape distinctive house-types. Particularly recognisable are the clusters of modest dwellings erected for the benefit of railway workers. This genre appeared in 1923 and eventually numbered over 1500. Their timber came from Railways Department land in the central North Island, cut to size in a factory at Frankton Junction. The houses all had very basic floor plans, disguised only by variably angled roofs and a selection of different front porches.

Home and hosed

Subdivision, 1950s.

'A nicely mown lawn'.

While still recovering from the Depression the New Zealand building industry was hit again — by the Second World War. Tradesmen were in short supply, as indeed were materials. Whereas tile and bitumen roofs had become rather fashionable, now there was little choice, for corrugated iron was simply unobtainable. An asbestos substitute appeared, but the traditional iron eventually returned with a vengeance, in a wide range of shapes and lengths.

By the 1950s the postwar shortages had eased and increased house construction was underway. The demand for new housing was insatiable, and subdivisions were gobbling up farmland on the edges of towns and cities. Soon New Zealand had one of the highest building rates in the world — achieving one house for every four citizens. But in spite of such activity our largest city had a population density of only a fraction of overseas equivalents. The national birthright, the quarter-acre section, had fuelled an urban sprawl of frightening proportions. Anywhere else on earth our barren backyards would have been considered wasteful. Eventually, a legal solution in the form of cross-leasing enabled these under-used garden plots and lawns to provide for a second wave of infill settlement.

Just as the electric tram had facilitated communities of villas, so did the automobile encourage suburban expansions in the '50s. By the end of the decade New Zealand was second only to the United States in per capita vehicle ownership. In the Auckland region this love affair with the car caused vehicle numbers to increase at a rate three times faster than the population. Perhaps the most graphic evidence of all was the Auckland Harbour Bridge itself. Built to service the North Shore it was the very stimulus for the further development of suburbia, and so it quickly needed its clip-on extension.

A growing sense of informality has encouraged open-plan living and a demand for decks, patios and pools. Their creation is often undertaken by the homeowner, who may be strapped for cash or else resent paying trademen's rates. More likely, however, he or she is responding to a deep-rooted do-it-yourself urge.

These weekend rituals have long

been a source of confusion to American visitors. Not only did the typical New Zealander not appear to take his career seriously enough, but he spent his two precious days off pouring his energy (often in the form of concrete) into his section.

Once land had been earmarked for a new subdivision it was instantly stripped of its topsoil. The landscape was reduced to inoffensive hillocks, soon to be cross-hatched with kerbs and channels and gently curving streets. To take advantage of any elevation some new houses could justify going split level, with the basement perhaps accommodating the second most important investment — the car(s). But as suburbs took to the hills, where even retaining walls were out of the question, a new technology was

needed. Thanks to the science of timber treatment, pole houses could now go where no dwelling had ventured before.

Technology meanwhile had also given our homes the benefits of 'permanent materials', meaning that they were impervious to rot (wet and dry) and borer. Corrugated iron may be eminently practical but it suffers from being somewhat common. 'Decramastic', however, gave the altogether classier look of a tile while retaining the advantages of iron — hidden beneath a crust of expoxy. Aluminium 'Ranchslider'-type doors could now provide reliable access to the patio or deck, rendering obsolete the old French doors. Finally, for something more upmarket than the ubiquitous weatherboard there was Summerhill Stone, truly a glamour

product. Made from a pink marble native to Canterbury, this 'concrete stone' was often also a feature of the lounge, where it constituted the family hearth.

When New Zealand's suburban sprawl was beginning in earnest in the 1950s, our inner cities were still largely intact. The changes arrived with the motorway, necessary to get the commuters downtown. Soon the old buildings began to crumble — at the hands of demolition gangs — and an inner-city renewal was underway. If the Californian bungalow was a gentle introduction to American architecture, there was no doubting the inspiration for the glass and concrete highrises crowding out our cities by the 1980s.

Home and hosed

With its moist, temperate climate, New Zealand grows grass well, if nothing else. Indeed the country's main earnings are derived from the highly efficient business of grass conversion. In suburbia, of course, with no herds or flocks to keep the grass down, the lawn becomes something of a preoccupation for most householders.

For many the home and garden is little short of a microcosm of the colonial estate of their forebears. With no need for actual bushcutting and clearing, today's suburban equivalent is rampant do-it-yourselfism, especially at weekends when the whine of mowers forms a background to the whirr of skillsaws, the repetition of hammer blows and engine noise as convoys of cars and trailers proceed to the local tip. Concrete paths, fences, decks, barbeques, renovations, painting are all grist to the mill of weekend industry.

A lot of the activity has to do with the country's main domestic building construction of wood and iron. Old villas and bungalows threaten an imminent return to the soil if not for suburban man and woman as Horatios on the bridge, battling against such an eventuality, slowing entropy and restoring order.

The garden and in particular the backyard is becoming less and less the domain it was a generation ago when, for instance, chook-runs were not uncommon. In a recent article, Australian writer Robin Ingram lamented the passing of the great backyard culture of Australia. His comments relate equally to this country, with the New Zealand reader making the appropriate substitutions of New Zealand for Australia, Masport for Victa, and so on.

'. . . I suspect we're all more products of our backyards than our backgrounds. And without wishing to appear like some patio Canute standing defiant against the encroaching New Waves, I can't help thinking that the products of the new backyard — the Lounge Lizard generation — will be missing out on a lot of basic yardcraft and Aussie ingenuity.

'To most of us, the Great Australian Outback was really only a quarter of an acre minus a three-bedroom brick bungalow and a moat of concrete. . . but it offered Lawrence of Suburbia at least as much adventure as Lawrence of

Surely no name is more familiar to New Zealand gardeners than Yates. And like another Kiwi brand success story, Edmonds Sure to Rise baking powder, Yates has also spawned a book — in this case the *Yates Garden Guide*, now with nearly a million copies sold since 1895.

The house of Yates goes back to 1879 and the arrival in New Zealand of Arthur Yates. An asthmatic, Yates had come to New Zealand to escape the chill of his hometown of Manchester, where his family were in business as seed merchants. While working on farms during his first few years in this country, Arthur Yates perceived the opportunities in local seed-supply and in 1883 founded Arthur Yates and Company in Auckland, the corporate predecessor of today's Yates NZ Ltd.

Within a few short years Arthur Yates and Co. had established itself as a successful enterprise. In 1911 a new six-storey head office was built in Lower Albert Street, which combined a retail outlet, rooftop plant nursery, seed-cleaning plant, packing plant and warehouse.

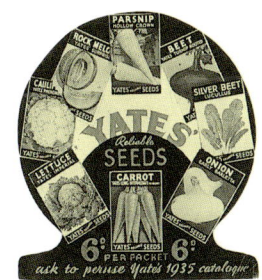

Arabia. Chook-runs with choko vines, the gang clubhouse under the sprawling jasmine, the smell of rubbish smouldering in 44-gallon incinerators, exotic, perfumed breezes wafting in off the compost heaps, and the din of Victa two-strokes sideswiping the Hills Hoists. Backyards had excitement, action and inexhaustible employment opportunities.

'Dads had a few rows of spuds and spinach and Mums had a corner in which flowers with names like delphinium, dahlia, stock and marigold contradicted her belief that variety was also the spice of garden design. And when domestic strife broke out over such complex issues as the way the hose was coiled, Dads would withdraw to musty back sheds containing tricycles and badminton sets from Christmasses past. The back shed was the refugee camp for the Dad in strife...a refuge from which to ponder life as a bastard until tea was ready.

'Dads have analysts now. Neighbours who haven't entirely covered the yard with cedar decking and sandstone pavers now sit down on rider mowers; chook sheds have become spa bath cabanas, and the incinerator has been replaced by a compost tumbler and set of recycling bins.

'Evolution has even interfered with those two sacred icons of Aussie suburbia, the Hills Hoist and the garden gnome....Many of you will know the slim odds of winning an argument against an architect. Tone Wheeler says yards are places where they herd sheep and cattle — and the old backyard was a corral where people penned in kids and dogs. Depressing places, he says, featuring a single steel tree — the Hills Hoist.

'Wheeler displays none of the other signs of an unhappy childhood, so I can only put his views down to an overdeveloped sense of aesthetics. But we have found common ground in the desirability of Australian suburbia retaining its rich diversity. For all the yuppifying of the suburbs that's going on, there's always one or two in the street who have failed to get the message. And that's not all bad.

'Maybe they can become our breeding stock. A dwindling National Treasure of self-sufficient Aussies who can not only live in their backyards, but off their backyards.

'While the Lounge Lizards are

Home and hosed

The international success of the kiwifruit is inextricably linked with the fruit and vegetable wholesaling company Turners and Growers. Edward Turner, a young English nurseryman, arrived in New Zealand in 1884. By the mid 1890s he had opened a wholesale fruit business in Auckland which in 1920 became Turners and Growers, the shareholders comprising members of Turner's family and the growers themselves. Harvey Turner, one of Edward Turner's nine sons, later ran the company as managing director for over 40 years and was responsible for pioneering exports of New Zealand-grown fruit and vegetables: the first fresh strawberries airfreighted to London, in the winter of 1946, and the first use of shipping containers.

It was at a company meeting in 1959 that the name 'kiwifruit' was coined to replace 'Chinese gooseberry'. It was an act that marked the greatest horticultural boom this country has ever seen. The name change was a response to problems in trying to launch the fruit on the huge and potentially highly profitable American market. Americans were wary of anything 'Chinese' and there was also confusion over the fruit's classification for duty. US import regulations subjected gooseberries to a high rate of duty, whereas the duty on items not specifically provided for was considerably lower. 'Kiwifruit' fitted the bill, while carrying through the New Zealand connection.

The rest is history. The next two decades saw kiwifruit — or 'kiwis' as they've now become in many overseas markets — harvested in their billions as European and North American markets responded with delight and enthusiasm to the exotic, tasty, green-fleshed fruit from downunder. Dozens of new recipes beyond its traditional use on pavlovas were concocted to use the new sensation.

reprogramming the solid–state controllers of their computerised irrigation systems, discouraging mozzies with their 15-watt electronic insect shields, changing filters in the fibreglass fountain and carp pond, and rearranging the patio furniture, the breeding stock can check the chooks and chokos, light a damp incinerator with a single match, change the plug in the Victa, and generally get on with learning the skills that made this country, well, able to get by.'

Characteristic of the New Zealand home garden in warmer districts are crops such as kiwifruit, tamarillo (a.k.a. tree tomato), feijoa and kumara. The kumara was among a number of food crops, including yam, taro and the gourd, brought to New Zealand by the first Polynesian settlers. Kumara was the most successful and indeed became the Maori's most important cultivated food, sustaining large concentrations of pa dwellers. It was grown throughout most of the North Island and in the South Island as far south as Banks Peninsula before cultivation was hindered by the cold. Some cultivations were huge — of 20 hectares or more.

The kiwifruit, of course, has made New Zealand horticulture internationally famous. The lowly Chinese gooseberry was renamed by Turners and Growers Ltd and promoted worldwide, proving a bonanza for scores of growers in the 1970s and early 1980s. Then the boom slowed and returns faded as other countries (many of them supplied with kiwifruit plants by New Zealanders!) began marketing their own crops. Similar attempts to exploit the feijoa and tamarillo and passionfruit — all of which add a distinctive subtropical flavour to northern gardens — have yet (if ever) to take off.

Gardening has from the first been a social activity and among the earliest of horticultural societies were those formed in Canterbury and New Plymouth. The first of those is home to one of our most notable public gardens, Ilam, created by a prominent Christchurch settler in the 1850s and brought to fame by Edgar Stead, horticulturist and ornithologist. During the 1920s Stead imported hundreds of rhododendrons and azaleas, and began a breeding programme which resulted in the creation of many new Ilam hybrids.

Early 20th century visitors to New

Zealand observed the spacious lawns of the new and sprawling suburbs. These green swards were usually sown as soon as the house was habitable and were conventionally a mixture of chewing fescue and browntop grasses. Fescues are known in the business as deep rooters and drought-resisters which make a good close bottom sward. Browntop, meanwhile, provides a durable turf. Generally a 2-to-1 fescue/browntop mixture does the job, but a quicker cover results with the addition of crested dogstail. True to its name, browntop has a tendency to brown off in summer. Provided there are no hosing restrictions, a good watering is often necessary during dry spells. For tougher surfaces, such as football fields, coarse and tufty ryegrass is called for. Also common is clover which remains green even over the driest summer.

A less desirable grass is paspalum, which smothers lawns and has seedheads resistant to certain mowers. It has to be forcefully evicted, its large flat crowns dug out, temporarily scarring the lawn surface. The tenacity of paspallum is shown by its love of even poor soils. On good land it cannot be eradicated, and a firmly established paddock of it is impossible to plough. Another unwelcome intrusion is kikuyu from Southern Rhodesia which sends out long runners and forms thick mats. However, it is ideal for sandy conditions and is therefore found in profusion at the beach, around camping grounds and baches.

Down on the farm, different soils and climates call for different pastures. The prudent farmer might therefore select a mixture of a dozen types of grass seed. In 1927, for example, the following assortment was suggested for sowing 'bush burn': chewings and meadow fescue, perennial and Italian ryegrass, crested dogstail, cocksfoot, timothy, meadow foxtail and five others.

Back on the home front the ever-growing lawn demands regular cutting. Lawn-mowers are categorised according to blade types — cylindrical or rotary. The former gives a scissor-like action and is preferred by the pefectionist. The older models were hand-powered with blades of varying number (from 3 to 5) and width (from 12 to 18 inches). In the 1920s some mowers boasted ball bearings, but all dragged a standard

Home and hosed

Our most famous mower had its origins in 1910, when two young New Zealand engineers, Rueben Porter and Harold Mason, went into business together in Greys Avenue, Auckland. Within a couple of years they had begun to manufacture vacuum pumps and a range of engines to power farm equipment. Mason and Porter Ltd, as the company was first registered, also involved itself in automobile and architectural engineering, but it was to be in the manufacture of lawn-mowers that 'Masport' became a household name.

In 1930 the company launched the first of its hand-push mowers, the Cleveland, named for Cleveland Road in the Auckland suburb of Parnell where the company then had its

premises. The first power-mower — a power-driven hand-mower — was introduced in 1938. An advance on the traditional wood-handle came with the 'super-streamlined' Meteor, whose twin tubular handles sported bicycle-like rubber grips. Soon the suburbs were buzzing to the sound of Lawnchief and Lawnsprite cylindricals and later the Rotacut rotary — not to be confused with the imported Rotocut.

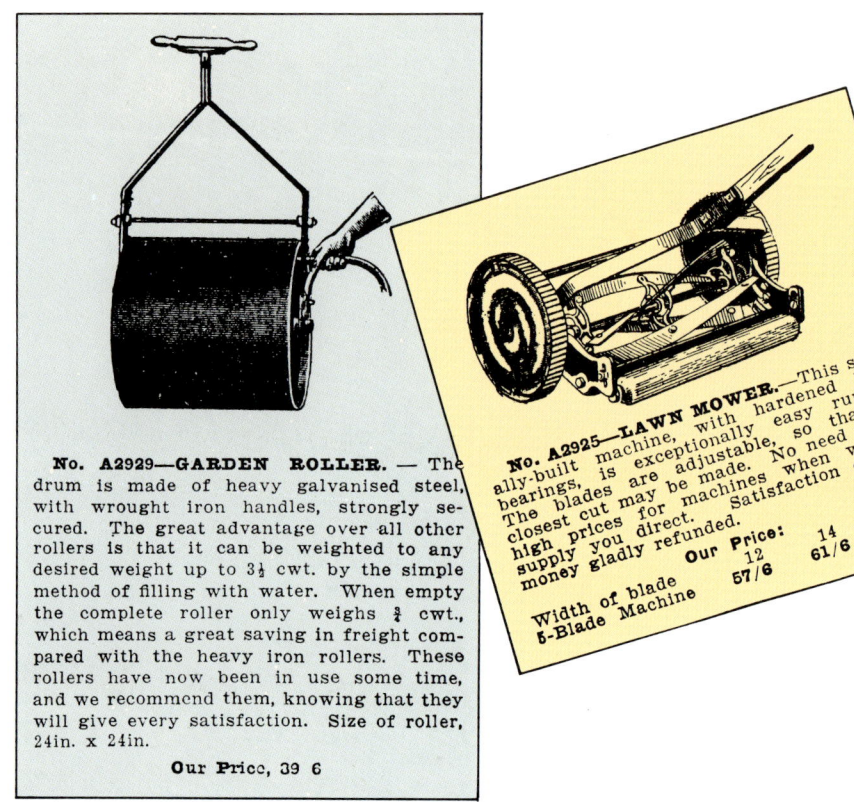

No. A2929—GARDEN ROLLER. — The drum is made of heavy galvanised steel, with wrought iron handles, strongly secured. The great advantage over all other rollers is that it can be weighted to any desired weight up to 3½ cwt. by the simple method of filling with water. When empty the complete roller only weighs ¾ cwt., which means a great saving in freight compared with the heavy iron rollers. These rollers have now been in use some time, and we recommend them, knowing that they will give every satisfaction. Size of roller, 24in. x 24in.

Our Price, 39 6

No. A2925—LAWN MOWER.—This specially-built machine, with hardened bearings, is exceptionally easy running. The blades are adjustable, so that closest cut may be made. No need to supply you direct. Satisfaction or money gladly refunded.

	Our Price:	
Width of blade	12	14
5-Blade Machine	57/6	61/6

catcher with sides of duck and a galvanised bottom. In 1929 models sold in New Zealand included the Gem, Colonial and Eureka, as well as the rather unusually-named Norka. The Farmers Trading Company of Auckland put their utilitarian 1936 Unity Special within the reach of every lawn-owner in the country — at 2/6 deposit and 1/9 per week for a year.

Alternatively, there was the Pennsylvania with patent 'Staytite' handle, or the top-of-the-line Richmond with five revolving blades of vanadium crucible steel. For larger lawns, such as bowling greens and tennis courts, there was the aristocratic Shanks's 1½ hp motorised Wizard — as used at Buckingham Palace. Also claiming Royal Appointment was another English maker,

Thomas Green, whose New Zealand agent was H. J. Ryan of Auckland. And therein lies a tale.

In the mid 19th century the Irish potato famine forced a young carpenter, Samuel Ryan, to sell up and emigrate. His timing wasn't the best, arriving as he did in Auckland just as New Zealand entered an eight-year-long depression. Not long after settling here, Ryan died, leaving a widow and four children. The eldest son, aged eight, was sent to work for a family who operated a business making heel-tips and toe-plates for boots. With this introduction to blacksmithing, Ryan junior later decided to set up by himself in Kingsland, Auckland. He charged 6/- for a set of four horseshoes, but extra if the animals were not broken in. After work he was particularly keen

on cricket, in pursuit of which he organised both a local team and a playing ground. Originally known as Walter's Paddock, this piece of land — covered with boulders and prone to flooding — soon became Ryan's Folly. Later still it was to become one of the most famous fields in the land — Eden Park.

Meanwhile the blacksmithy had failed but, undaunted, Ryan and his three teenage sons tried again, in a tiny shop in St Paul Street. They returned to the business Ryan had learned as a child — making boot-protectors. Some of the necessary machinery was ordered from Australia but other vital tools had to be hand-made on the premises. This was not the only shortage. Obtaining steel from England so soon after the First World War

The Masport "Cleveland"

In response to the popular demand for a large wheel mower, we now introduce the Masport "Cleveland," with 10in. x 1⅛in. driving wheels.

As in other models, the spiral blades are made from oil tempered and hardened Sheffield steel. The bearings are of the cup and cone adjustable type with a double coil spring at the ends of the cylinder shaft to take up adjustment in a simple manner. This machine gives an exceptionally low cut.

Made in two sizes only:—

14in. Ball Bearing	- - -	**77/6**
16in. Ball Bearing	- - -	**82/6**

Finish—Gold and Blue.

The Masport "Cleveland" can be supplied with rubber-tyred driving wheels, which is the very latest innovation and assists in the elimination of noise when the mower is being wheeled on concrete paths or when in actual use.

In two sizes only:—

14in. Ball Bearing	- - -	**87/6**
16in. Ball Bearing	- - -	**92/6**

Finish—Gold and Blue.

Obtainable from all Hardware Dealers.

was almost impossible. Kiwi ingenuity saved the day and the Colonial Sugar Refinery's tip at Chelsea provided the solution. Steel strapping from jute bales was straightened and annealed and turned into Clematis-brand Heel Armour.

After the Second World War the Ryans branched out into lawn-mowers and produced their Speedicut. This elegant cylindrical mower rolled lawns as it mowed them and in 1953 cost £78.

The face of lawn-mowing was altered radically one afternoon in 1952 when, in Concorde, NSW, Australia, one Mervyn Victor Richardson connected a small petrol motor to a rotary blade and so gave birth to the world's first rotary mower. Conventional cylindrical mowers are mostly defeated by the coarse lawn grasses — paspalum for one — which dominate much of Australian and New Zealand suburbia and the greater cutting power of the rotary proved an immediate hit. Christening his invention the 'Victa', Mervyn Richardson opened a factory the following year to manufacture his new mower and within five years had sold 100,000 machines.

Other lawn-mower manufacturers were quick to recognise the potential of the rotary. Ryan's responded with the first distinctive mower designed for local conditions — the Speediescythe. This no-nonsense rotary mower, half the price of its older brother, was intended to deal with paspalum. It was basically just a motorised slasher, powered by an English JAP engine. The latter was war surplus and originally designed as a power unit for air-raid shelters.

NEW ZEALAND-made

Masport

RAPID BALL BEARING

2/6 PER WEEK

Home and hosed

Flemings of Gore began life as a miller of choice Southland oats, first producing traditional oatmeal and, later, rolled oats and their famous Creamota. For much of the first half of this century, Creamota was known as the national breakfast. Thousands of youngsters used to scrape the bottoms of their breakfast bowls on winter mornings to find a porcelain picture of Sergeant Dan, the Creamota Man. From the 1920s to the 1950s good old Sergeant Dan was elevated almost to the status of folk hero, his vim and vigour attributed to the healthy qualities of Creamota — 'best for breakfast, body and brain'.

Never far from the public eye as a source of nutrition, oats have lately achieved a higher

Sgt Dan.

profile with the increasing awareness of diet and good health. They are an excellent source of soluble dietary fibre and their consumption assists in lowering blood cholesterol. Healthy sales of milled and rolled oats make the continuation of Southland's oatfields assured.

Nothing remains the same, not even breakfast. Traditionally, New Zealand's first — and possibly most important — meal of the day was a major event. A bowl of porridge was followed by a laden plate of bacon, eggs and toast, all washed down with a pot of tea. The real working man even dispensed with the small goods in favour of something meatier, like mince or chops. Today, however, the demands on time and a growing awareness of diet have forced a change. The modern breakfast is wholesome, but speedy.

Historically, the most persistent item on the New Zealand breakfast table has been oats. Originally grown for the benefit of horses, this cereal was sometimes processed as a sideline by flourmills. But the ideal growing conditions of Southland and the southern appetite for the traditional Scots' breakfast soon ensured its popularity. Although a seasonal taste, oats have survived the changing times. Since the arrival of the first commercial muesli, Vita Crunch, in 1975, oat sales have skyrocketed. One-third of the nation's oats enters the market inside muesli packets.

The company which has cornered the oat market is Flemings, flourmillers and cerealmillers in Gore since 1878 and now producers of 90 percent of the nation's porridge. For much of the first half of this century porridge was personified by a boy-scout — Sergeant Dan — who graced Creamota packets through to the 1940s.

At this stage the young sergeant had

I am the man, says Sergeant Dan,
I care not one iota,
For who can be, as strong as me,
While I have my Creamota.

a decided military look, with lemon squeezer hat and a toy rifle in the sloped arms position. It was appropriate therefore that the country's first oats were also patriotic, known as the 'Onwards' strain.

Flemings' 'cream o' the oat' may now be the clear market leader, but it has had competition. At the turn of the century one could prepare Cameron's Moa brand 'Wheatina' rolled wheat, or alternatively, Heather brand 'Ambrosia' rolled wheat from the Carlyle Mills of Christchurch. Meanwhile, in Auckland the Northern Roller Milling Co. had its

With smaller families, televison and a faster pace of life, the formal morning mealtime has been replaced by a type of communal grazing. But still a feature of the first meal of the day is the kitchen radio, whose breakfast sessions reflect the changing times. The singing commercial arrived on New Zealand radio in the late forties and soon the country was being serenaded with sing-along jingles about tea, petrol and plumbing, and dental problems. Taranaki listeners were familiar with:

So give your plumber or builder a call,
He'll tell you 'Stanley' engineers are really on the ball.

Auckland's most popular jingle — and, in fact, the country's favourite — was that advertising an Auckland dental technician, to the tune of Clementine:

Broke my dentures, broke my dentures,
Woe is me, what shall I do?
Take them in to Mr Geddes,
And he'll fix them, just like new.
What's the address? What's the address?
Hurry please, and tell me do,
Top of Queen Street, on the corner,
And the number's four-nine-two.

So well known did the song become, you could be sure of hearing it sung at raucous gatherings wherever Kiwis might be, from New Year's Eve celebrations in London to Munich beerfests.

flag-waving Standard range of oaten products, in addition to Germina and Semolina wheat derivatives.

Also to be found on the national breakfast table in the 1920s were Kellogg's All Bran, New Oata and Pep. Another American company was Post's, who provided us with Bran Flakes and Toasties. Or, if you preferred, Gerstina, Grape Nuts, Gruelmeal, Oatina, Oatienuts, Ota and even Breakfast D'Light.

By 1920 the science of breakfast nutrition had arrived. Milk Oaties were 'partially steam cooked by the exclusive Thistle process which Dextrinises the starch'. Preparation time was also down — to one minute — with Diamond O-TIS, the energy breakfast which conveniently delivered 'all the foodstuffs essential to life'. It was a product of the Timaru Milling Company which had begun in 1883. Diamond was born when a South Canterbury farmer, James Bruce, chose it as a trademark for his Silverdust flour. Later, when he became part of the Timaru Milling Company, his distinctive red motif was retained, appearing first for Diamond oatmeal. Then, in the 1940s, it was emblazoned on macaroni packets when New Zealand responded to another foreign influence and produced its first pasta. Today the company operates as New Zealand Cereal Foods Ltd — yet another division of Goodman Fielder Wattie.

The health-conscious breakfast goes back even further than the 1920s in the case of Sanitarium. In the 19th century sanitariums were places where the infirm retreated to recuperate. However, in Michigan the name was adopted by a health food company which was to extend its benevolence to New Zealand in 1900. Fully owned and operated by the Seventh-Day Adventist Church, the Sanitarium Company now practises its maxim that 'Health is Wealth' from three factories. Two of its products are household names above all others, and one — Weet-Bix — is our most popular breakfast cereal of all. In 1988 it was the 13th best-selling foodstuffs brand, just heading off Wattie's spaghetti.

Weet-Bix has captured more than 40 percent of the country's cereal market — hardly surprising given that some people eat it for breakfast, lunch and dinner.

Home and hosed

Sir Edmund Hillary chooses WEET-BIX

Sir Edmund Hillary took Weet-Bix with him on his famous Himalayan expedition. For the same reason, too — because Weet-Bix is so delicious, so full of nourishing goodness, so quick and easy to serve it's with the New Zealand Antarctic expedition. Have your Weet-Bix with hot milk. It's the perfect winter breakfast.

And here's another Weet-Bix scoop — the story of flight on 50 full-colour picture cards

Fifty free full-colour cards tell the exciting story of the "Evolution of Flight". There are two cards in every large 24-ounce packet of Weet-Bix; one in the 12-ounce size. Start collecting them today.

With about 40 percent of the breakfast cereal market, Weet-Bix is consumed by the tonne every day, an awesome 361,000,000 Weet-Bix each year. For an idea of just how many that is, imagine them laid end to end in a straight line and then driving along that line at 100 kph day and night. It would be nearly 13 days before you passed the last one.

New Zealand is rich in tales of extraordinary Weet-Bix consumption and of feats and habits that constitute a cereal subculture. Sanitarium's archive contains, among others, one letter from a concerned daughter whose father polished off a packet a day. Boys' boarding schools, not usually noted for dining-room etiquette, have also produced some record Weet-Bix appetites. Eating the biscuits dry, without the assistance of milk, was perhaps the toughest challenge.

Beyond our shores, Weet-Bix is also made in Australia, and about 57 tonnes finds its way around the Pacific each year.

In its early days Weet-Bix's malted whole wheat biscuits were not intended just for morning consumption, but were

'Ideal For Every Meal'. Nowadays 'whole wheat' displaces 'malted' in importance as the flaky biscuits have responded, subtly, to changing times. Weet-Bix and its Sanitarium stablemate Bran-Bix and Grain Products' Vita Brits are all manufactured from cooked whole wheat grains which have been rolled and press-moulded into shape. Similar is Sanitarium's Granose and its non-survivor, Bixies. Other processes provided further variations on grain, from minor explosions (Puffed Wheat, Ricies and Honey Puffs) to straight flakes (Frosties and Kornies). The last category once included Weeties made by Cereal Foods in Grey Lynn, Auckland and Sydenham, Christchurch. This company also introduced the original Kornies, 'Everybody's Breakfast', still around but

now owned by Sanitarium-related Grain Products.

A popular and long-standing feature of breakfast cereals is the free giveaway. Such inducements probably began with cigarette cards but have since been employed by all types of products. At least one New Zealand ornithologist received early encouragement from bird cards in Gregg's 'fuller flavoured' jelly packets. More original was the 3-D series put out by Bell tea in about 1954. This set of 50 views, heavily biased towards the recent Royal Visit, was the first of its type produced in this country. However, most consistently generous with free gifts has been the Sanitarium Company.

In the 1940s they launched their *Treasury of the Years*, an extensive picture panorama that ran to at least

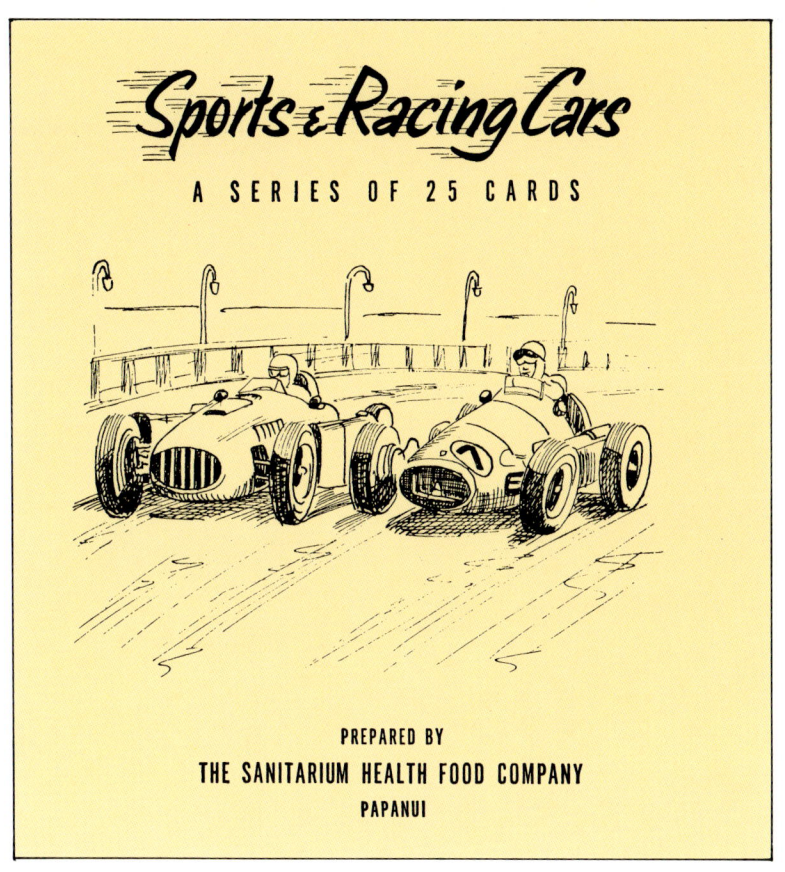

Sports & Racing Cars

A SERIES OF 25 CARDS

PREPARED BY

THE SANITARIUM HEALTH FOOD COMPANY

PAPANUI

DISCOVERY

H.M.S. "LION"

four albums and 200 cards. They came with Granose, Bixies, Weet-Bix and San Bran, with the larger 24 oz packets providing two cards. Later came the encyclopaedic *Wonder Book of General Knowledge* with its set of 60. A swap department was set up at the Papanui factory to assist the collector. Any three surplus cards would bring, by return post, the card of one's choice. In the late '50s, the postwar baby–boomers — especially the boys — were well catered for with regular sets featuring racing cars, ships and aircraft.

There have been other types of novelties as well. In the early 1950s the Kellogg's Corn Flakes packet featured cut-out masks, thus making storage difficult if the young consumer became impatient. Plastic model racing cars

(with real wheels) and cowboys were popular. But most ingenious, and timely, was the miniature submarine which, with a bit of baking soda, could emulate the *Nautilus* under the polar ice-cap and dive on demand.

Another Sanitarium product stimulated a competitor which became a New Zealand institution. But even more colourful perhaps are its true origins — a combination of German chemistry and a South American meat surplus. During the 1840s millions of Europeans emigrated in search of a better life, and many of those who stayed behind were to remain hungry. Justus Liebig, however, devised a scheme to assist the malnourished. He developed a concentrated extract of meat which took advantage of the cattle population of Uruguay, previously only

exploited for its hides. 'Extractum Carnis Liebig' was thus born and came to Britain in 1865. But at the turn of the century this beef extract gained the name by which it is still known: Oxo. In the meantime a famous competitor appeared in the form of Bovril, invented by a Scotsman in Canada. Obviously, meat substitutes were rather unnecessary in New Zealand in view of its own (live) bovine stock. However, there were local extracts of meat produced by Wellington's Gear Company and the Christchurch Meat Company, for example. Hellaby's of Auckland and a Dunedin manufacturer were a little more cheeky with their Bovo and Bovine respectively, while Carnox — obviously for carnivores — beef essence from the P & O Manufacturing Co. of Wellington, in

Home and hosed

Whatever your preference for yeast extract — whether Marmite or Vegemite — there is no doubt that the spreads are something of an acquired taste. Popularity is highest in countries with a British influence where, it can be argued, life's subtleties — which include cricket, as well as yeast extracts spread thinly (early Marmite jars carried the advice: 'Too much spoils the flavour') — are more appreciated. Any success the novel taste of Vegemite or Marmite might have expected in the world's biggest novelty market, the United States, was stymied at the outset due to the Americans' insistence on spreading the stuff as they do their peanut butter and jelly ... with predictable results. In India, meanwhile, locally made Marmite — a heritage from the days of the Raj — carries the legend: 'For toast, sandwiches and chapattis.'

the 1920s, was as close as we got to Oxo.

Extracts of meat were meant to be wholesome substitutes for those who couldn't get the real thing. Otherwise there was always Marmite. This distinctive dark brown concentrate, originally from the Marmite Food Extract Company of 59 Eastcheap, London, was first registered in New Zealand and Australia in 1910 — the same year, incidentally, that the Oxo cube was introduced to the world. Bearing its ornamental stock-pot trademark, English-made Marmite was exported to this country until about 1930. Then, for a few years, it was mixed with local product, until the '40s when New Zealand began manufacturing its very own version.

There seems now to have been an element of confusion concerning Marmite's make-up. While at times Marmite described itself variously as a yeast or vegetable extract, there was never at any time any meat involved. There is something of a continuing myth that Marmite contains meat while its main competitor, Vegemite, does not. The irony is that Marmite's New Zealand manufacturers, Sanitarium, are Seventh-Day Adventist and therefore vegetarian. However, for extra reassurance, today's Marmite jar now states: 'contains no animal products'.

If Oxo had inspired Marmite, then the latter was responsible for Vegemite. In 1923 an Australian, Fred Walker, planned to compete with the English spread. The chief scientist in his company, Dr Cyril Callister, devised a thick dark paste combining yeast from Carlton & United Breweries with, among other things, celery and onions. In a play on words this new product was named Parwill, implying that although 'Ma might', 'Pa will.' Unfortunately such obscure originality wasn't appreciated and so the persistent Walker sought public assistance. A competition was won by Vegemite, which soon became available in this country.

It was first made here in 1958 and is now produced by Kraft Foods. Although invented across the Tasman — with a plaque marking the site of the original Melbourne factory — Vegemite is actually more popular here in New Zealand. Kiwi's consume 330 grams per person per year (representing 2,200,000 jars), a full 30 grams more than the average Aussie.

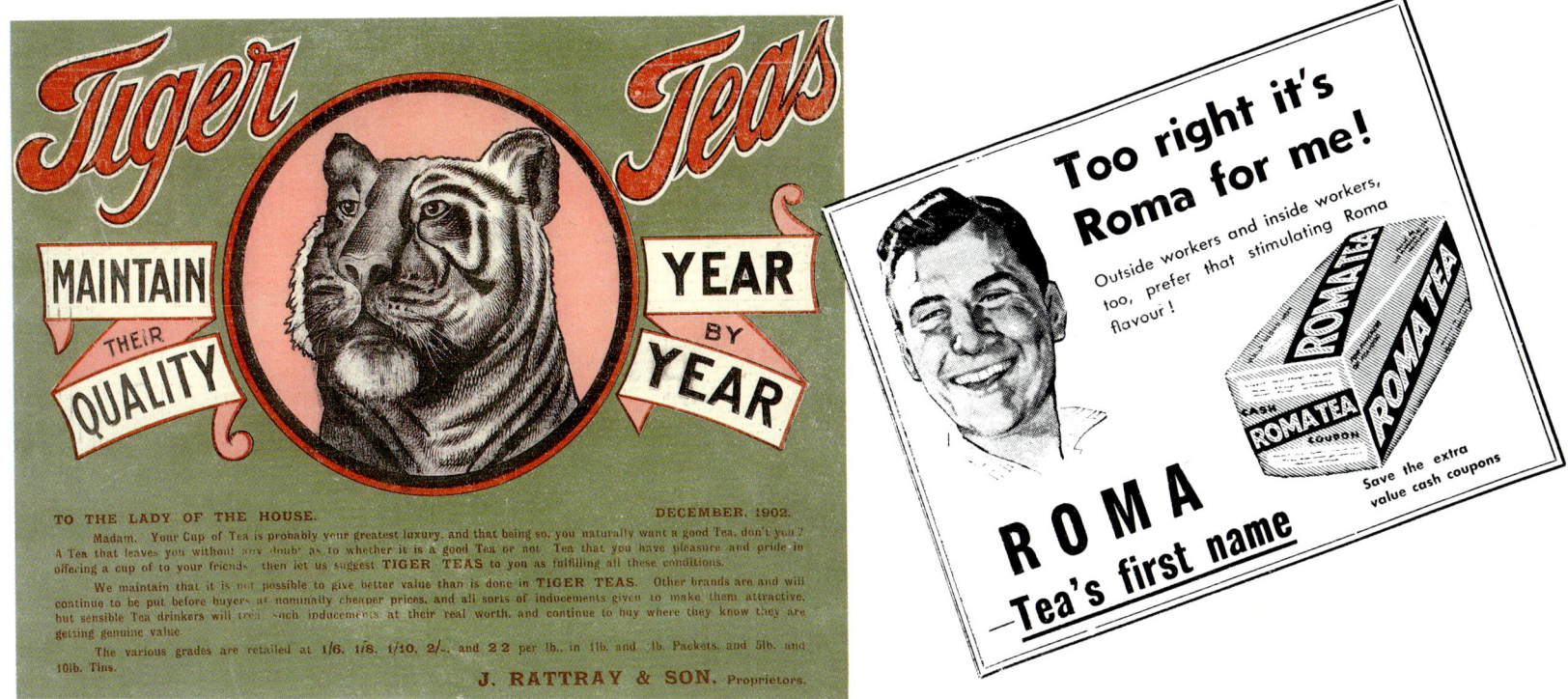

Wherever the English settled they took tea. A universal panacea, a good cup of tea could both warm one up and cool one down, as required. It was the obvious refreshment in times of stress and, further, the universal pick-me-up was safe, even back in 1908 when Satura D blend claimed to 'stimulate without injury' and would not 'hurt the children'.

Certain early brands of tea are still household names in New Zealand. Others have disappeared including a bit of a mouthful to ask for in 1897 — Brown Barrett and Co's Colombo Garden Heliotrope label. Alternatively, their Lion Brand Blue label claimed a 'thick, full, fine liquor' — presumably of the non-spiritous type. For the true connoisseur L. D. Nathan's Standard teas of 1899

came in eight different blends — 'all perfectly distinctive in character'.

Photographs of inner-city Auckland in the early 1900s reveal corner stores prominently advertising Nelson Moates and Suratura Teas. If this wasn't enough the customer could still choose between Rava, Raven, Rival and Roma! A feature of the early days was the large selection available. Auckland, for example, supported some 30 tea merchants as recently as 1940, but by 1988 there were not even 10.

In 1933 New Zealand was drinking 200 million cups of Bell tea per year. Two years later the unusual Mazawattee was proudly claiming to be 'The World's Best Tea' and that 'Doctors and Analysts Recommend it'. Nevertheless, it was Bell that survived, to become the national

bestseller in 1988 with 30 percent of the market.

Another big seller in the early '30s was the homely Mother Hubbard. Auckland's Farmers Trading Company moved over 200,000 lbs of this blend in three years. In memory of pioneering days they could supply their teas in 2 lb, 3 lb and 6 lb billies. Serious drinkers might prefer the cheaper Fannings line, available in real bulk — 60 lb half-chests. Much more exclusive was the Kozie brand of 1908, 'an ideal tea for refined homes'.

The 1920s and '30s saw the arrival, and departure, of many brands — Biplane, Gold Leaf and Sunkist teas among them. But one with real impact was imported from Australia in 1937, and was the subject of New Zealand's first

Home and hosed

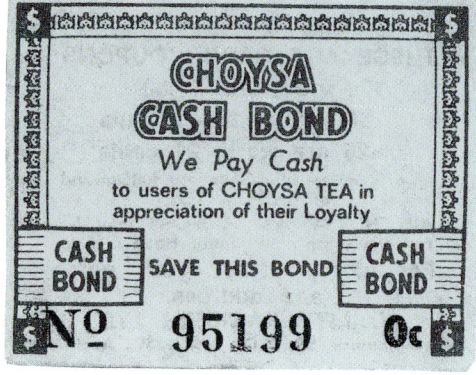

Over the years the nation's tea-drinkers have been wooed by various jingles and claims. Roma was 'dust free' and Bell was the 'quality tea with the guarantee'. As an added inducement, and 'to users in appreciation of their loyalty', cash coupons have long been associated with tea. Generally, in the '60s and '70s, these were redeemable for about one cent each, although some more demanding merchants required them in multiples of 50.

radio jingle. So popular was it that sheet music was provided for the benefit of dance bands. In addition to this free advertising, Bushell's was enthusiastically endorsed by one of the country's great radio personalities — Aunt Daisy herself. But stiff competition was to come with Choysa, a brand first introduced in the early 1900s by Auckland's Bond Brothers — Enos, Elon and Enoch. With its bright oval logo, Choysa was, in the '50s, the first tea to be marketed nationwide. Today it is second only to Bell in national sales.

If the Second World War American serviceman travelled the world in search of a good cup of coffee, then his New Zealand counterpart was equally adamant in sticking to his 'cuppa'. *Kalimera Kiwi*, a New Zealand soldier's account of the campaigns in Egypt and Greece, tells of the standard soldier's lunch in the Egyptian desert: a half-tin of bully beef per man and 'the ubiquitous, but ever-welcome, cup of tea'. What's more, the Kiwis even had an ingenious, if strictly forbidden, method of brewing up: a half-gallon of precious petrol poured into a hollow in the sand and ignited, thereby enabling a cup of water to be boiled, literally, in half a tick.

In the late 1960s the Tea Council of New Zealand campaigned to create a new awareness of tea. This was aimed unashamedly at the youth market and used one-time pirate radio station Hauraki for leverage. DJ Ian Magan admitted to personally taking at least six cups per day while Sandy Edmonds, an antipodean Sandi Shaw and star of television's *C'mon*, endorsed iced tea. 'Tea Raves' were presented to a generation who were probably more interested in something a little stronger than tannin.

To counteract the growing fruit juice and aerated beverage threat in New Zealand the tea industry diversified. Tea bags, in either string or tag form, have proved increasingly popular, particularly in the Auckland region, but old habits die hard and there is still traditional loyalty to leaf tea in the South Island.

American military personnel posted to New Zealand during the Second World War were warned of the difficulty of finding an acceptable cup of coffee. This, they were advised, was only available in camp as one of the characteristics

Bushells

MRP

ESSENCE OF COFFEE & CHICORY
SWEETENED

Contains NOT LESS THAN 50% COFFEE ESSENCE

the New Zealanders shared with the British was a complete inability to make coffee. Although this American presence encouraged its popularity, coffee had in fact been around in New Zealand for at least 60 years.

Perhaps the earliest local manufacturer, and a name still associated with the beverage, was William Gregg of Dunedin. He was a coffee-roaster in 1861 and his Club brand dates from about 1880. Competition came from another Dunedinite, Alexander Durie, who supplied not only Thistle, Rose and Shamrock coffees, but also Bourbon brand for continental preferences. Further south was David Strang of Invercargill, whose patent hot-air process gave 'the purest roasted coffee known' and won prizes on both sides of the

Tasman at exhibitions in the '80s. His Gold Medal Maori brand was still around in the 1920s, claiming to be the economic alternative to tea.

At the time of the First World War, L. D. Nathan of Auckland introduced the mystique of the Middle and Near East into coffee with its Empress, Khedive and Sultan brands. Much of this early coffee was necessarily adulterated by the addition of chicory, a perennial plant with a lengthy taproot. Economics and the availability of coffee beans resulted in various additives, including acorns and parsnip roots. Chicory was surely preferable to these and New Zealand drinkers could at least take heart from the fact that their adulterant was locally grown and world class. A parsnip look-alike, chicory does particularly well in

parts of Otago and Canterbury where various coffee merchants had plantations. Trent Bros of Christchurch claimed to be Australasia's chicory pioneers, and won an award for their product at the 1873 Vienna Exhibition.

A touch of class was given to coffee drinking at the end of the 19th century with the provision of coffee palaces. New Plymouth, for example, boasted the Grand Central Coffee Palace and Sea Side Resort. However, this term needs to be seen alongside such other euphemisms of the day as 'boot palaces' (footwear shops), 'Polytechnic' (a ready-made draper in Oamaru), various 'emporiums' (markets) and even a 'City Hatoneum' (a Dunedin hat shop).

In 1907 W. Gregg & Co. claimed their Club brand coffee had 'practically

Home and hosed

**A selection of
Wellington and Christchurch
coffee bars
from the mid 1960s**

Americano Coffee Lounge
Balalaika Coffee Lounge
Beachcomber Coffee Lounge
Cafe Capri Coffee Lounge
Casa Pepe
Chez Paree
Colorado Coffee Bar
Drift Inn Coffee Lounge
El Segundo Coffee Lounge
Estrellita Coffee Lounge
Expresso Coffee Shop
Fabriola Coffee Parlour
Fondella Coffee Shop
Grotto Coffee Bar
Hawaiin Coffee Lounge
Intermezzo Coffee Lounge
La Scala

monopolised the trade from the North Cape to Stuart Island'. Its distinctive airtight cannister and wrapper were familiar sights. . .as was the square Bushells bottle in the early 1950s.

After the Second World War, ground coffee became unobtainable, prompting the launch of Bushell's Essence of Coffee and Chicory. This product's red and blue label portrayed an unknown Middle Eastern identity with beard and fez.

Coffee essence has now given way to instant coffee, a product dominated in this country by the multinational Nestlé Company. The Swiss giant responded to massive Brazilian coffee surpluses in the 1930s by developing 'Nescafe', one of the world's first instant-food products. This convenient beverage was part of the American GI's daily ration kit and first

appeared in the grocery stores of New Zealand in the late '40s.

Old Mill is a local brand dating back to 1898 and a Queen Street grocer, Mr Smeaton. After his death the stylised windmill trademark was sold to Hutchinson's who had a chain of groceries around the city.

As a social drink coffee mirrors the times. In the 1920s the focus was the soda fountain, a source of fizzy drinks and ice-cream sundaes. That institution was replaced in the next decade by the milkbar. In time, this also was supplanted in social desirability by the coffee bar. So, 60 years after the days of the coffee palaces, the beverage was back, modernised. Now it reflected a growing awareness of other, non-British cultures. The very names of New Zealand's

'As close as one could get to the real thing.'

numerous coffee bars in the '60s were a pot-pourri of exotica, with continental Europe particularly favoured. There were La Scalas, Sorrentos, Gi-Gis, Piccolos and Rios and, for the artistically inclined, a Lautrec and Picasso. Apart from new ways with coffee, the expresso machine at the Milano, for example, brought many patrons something else — an introduction to modern Italian design. Until 'OE' really took off, these places were as close as one could get to the real thing.

Their interiors were classic stereotypes, from suspended strings ceilings to hessian wall-coverings with chianti bottles and glass Japanese fishing floats for decoration. Also to be expected were collages of posters and record covers.

The lot of the conscientious house-keeper was far from easy in the early days of European settlement. While a farm was being wrestled from native bush one's first home in the antipodes was often temporary, of raupo and nikau. The Maori had developed this technique and could quickly arrange such a weatherproof structure. Alternatively there was the slab house, of split logs affixed to corner posts which were rammed into the ground. These shelters were only required until a more durable weatherboarded house could be built — preferably before the next winter. Then the slab house could revert to another use, perhaps as a stable or cowshed.

But back in the new homestead there were still discomforts to endure,

such as the intrusion of dust in the summer and mud in the winter. Although there were no real labour-saving appliances to speak of, there was help at hand — if one could afford it. At the beginning of the 20th century there were nearly 20,000 domestic servants in New Zealand, and still not enough to satisfy the demand. 'Nugget' floor polish alluded to this in 1922 with an advertisement claiming it 'solves the servant problem'. This scarcity could be attributed to the customary hours of work, often long in the extreme. Further, there were no guaranteed holidays.

Before the comparatively uncluttered lines of the modern interior, dust had a field-day. Everywhere there were ledges to catch it and textures to ensnare it. Innumerable ornaments, from trophy

heads to picture frames, demanded daily attention. It was an exhaustive business, requiring dust sheets over the furniture to prevent further spreading of the problem. The Kapai Corn Broom Company of Auckland produced the tools for the job in the early 1900s — at the rate of 100,000 units per annum. There were brooms for all parts of the house, from spiral chimney sweepers to long-handled cobweb removers and verandah scrubbers. Bannister brushes and brooms were variously composed of fibre, bristle or hair, while American corn whisks guaranteed an even better sweep.

Corn brooms came in many models in the 1920s, including the well-named Shaker (2/5), Ruru (3/11), Tui (4/4) and, top of the range, the Kiwi (4/11). For the kitchen stove there were other varieties,

Home and hosed

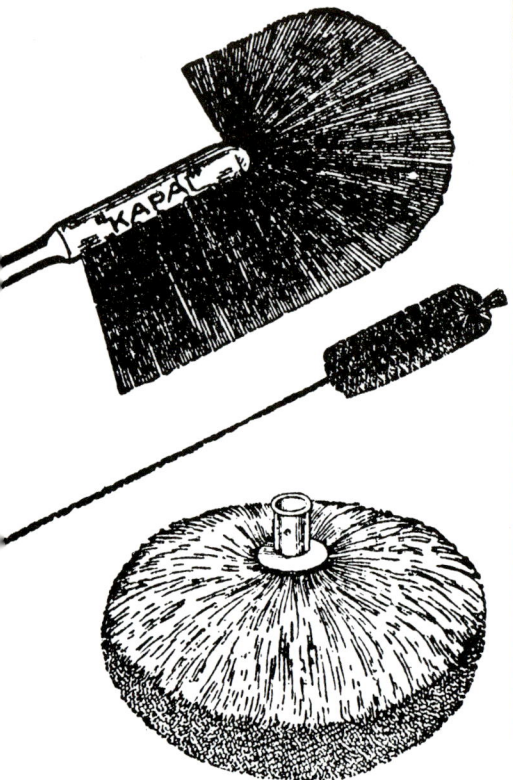

H6070.

H6080.

H6100.

H6120.

from bristling scrubbers for vigorous polishing to round types for applying blacklead. Eventually Kapai brooms disappeared, just like the Auckland-made boots of the same name. Buntings became synonymous with brushes, whose bristles became increasingly of nylon. Spik presumably kept our houses spick and span and the itinerant Bon Brush man delivered them to our door.

The floor was of course the natural home for dirt. There were all manner of commercial solutions to the problem but none alleviated the need for elbow-grease. At least with the arrival of floor coverings the nature of the job changed somewhat. Congoleum, for example, was waterproof, unaffected by mopping, sanitary, vermin-proof and guaranteed

not to curl at the edges. It was a printed felt-based material with an extra heavy colour coating and superior to the cheapest grades of the alternative, linoleum. However, in the 1920s the best lino appeared to be the superior floor covering. American-made and 9/11 per yard it came in a wide range of patterns, with Oriental designs simulating tiles and carpets predominating. It was intended for all rooms of the house, even the bedroom, where the coldness and hardness of its 'dainty. . .blue carpet pattern', for example, would be countered with a rug. For the hall there was passage linoleum in widths of 36, 45 and 54 inches. If one's hall was slightly wider than any of these, then the usual practice was to cunningly paint or stain the exposed floorboards.

The initial maintenance of linoleum consisted of a coating of varnish. To make for easier polishing thereafter a handy hint was to swab the lino with stale cold tea.

As villas were superseded by bungalows, passages either shrank or became vestibules. In the mid '30s the Farmers Trading Company of Auckland could only offer passage linoleum in two modest widths — 27 and 36 inches. But by now there were also carpets to choose from, with such names as Axminster, Wilton and Brussels. Like the early linos these were highly patterned and had elaborate borders, but stopped well short of the skirting boards — unlike the wall-to-wall carpets of today.

Early New Zealand-made carpets followed the English tradition — hardly

The Feeny VACUUM CLEANER

"UNQUESTIONABLY THE BEST"

surprising given that many of the factory staff were imported from Kidderminster. Axminster designs proved particularly popular, in florals, persians, autumn tones and contemporary patterns, but original schemes based on New Zealand native flora were also introduced. Less expensive were jute hearth rugs, woven grass runners and coconut matting.

The 1930s had also seen the appearance of locally produced Tattersfield rugs with decidedly art deco designs, woven in Auckland from pure New Zealand wool. As well, home furnishers prior to the Second World War could take advantage of another New Zealand manufacture — Feltex — a thick mottled felt that provided economical all-over 'carpeting'. At the Lower Hutt factory of Felt & Textiles of New Zealand

Ltd, greasy wool was progressively carded, felted and pounded to give results of varying grades. As well as floor coverings the felt was used for slippers, millinery goods and even as anti-vibration mountings for heavy machinery.

All of these floor coverings were further dust traps. At least the early carpet-sweepers kept the maid — or housewife — up off her knees. With roller bearings and brushes of Chinese bristles these labour-savers were thrust backwards and forwards to uplift the dirt. By pressing a lever — preferably well clear of the house — the trapped dust and microbes could be safely disposed of. These basic appliances were usually green in colour and had such impressive names as Monarch, Empire,

Success and Conquest.

For improved housekeeping there was the electric vacuum cleaner, used extensively in New Zealand by the mid '20s. In 1935 electricity consumers in Auckland were told this device was 'the greatest help any housewife can have' and 'a fine investment in health'. For loyal citizens that year the Auckland Farmers Trading Company offered the 'British Empire' electric vacuum cleaner and the 1950s brought the Silent Electrix Vatric and Goblin Wizard. It was an improvement on the latter, called the Goblin Ace, first produced here in 1948 by Fisher & Paykel, that became perhaps the best known vacuum cleaner of all. Its extensive set of attachments included an upholstery tool and crevice nozzle, and a container of 'Goblin Deofume'

Home and hosed

SCOURINE.

Reckitt & Colman's most successful cleanser has been its most original. It was perhaps inspired by the English Harpic, named by its inventor Harvey Pickup. Thus was born Janola, the brainchild of two Aucklanders who named it in honour of their wives — Jan and Nola. However, it now competes in a market where speed is of the essence. At present the market is dominated by Jif — applied in a jiffy. There is also a male equivalent of the old Clever Mary, Handy Andy, launched by Lever Brothers in 1959.

crystals provided a 'pleasant disinfectant vapour during use'.

Eradicating dirt has always been a serious business — the original germ warfare. Such concern for hygiene and health was not surprising in 1918 when nearly 7000 New Zealanders died from a virulent strain of influenza. Pearson's carbolic sandsoap was mindful of infection. Its makers claimed in 1951 that it 'destroys all insect life'. Even more potent was Sopo — in 1920 it was the self-claimed 'King of grease destroyers'.

A vital ingredient of many of the early soaps was carbolic, something of a wonder chemical in its day. But in the unlikely event of failure there were even stronger measures, such as Kerol, an imported British disinfectant. In 1922 it was claimed it 'kept plague away' and

was '24 times stronger than carbolic acid'. Carbolic was to be found in Pumicine compressed sandsoap, first produced in 1906 by Edward Firth of Mt Eden. A more famous Firth was Josiah who introduced his 'calcined sterilised pumice' for insulation in 1897. Still a big name in building materials Firth began business by putting pumice to its other washday application — as a constituent in the concrete surrounds for copper boilers.

Pumice, a volcanic byproduct, was also a component of many soaps. From about 1895 there was the sanitary Sanative, Cyclone — 'best on earth' — in 1905, and Laborlite — 'your washword' — in 1922. In the 1920s there was also Karbol and Olo-Pum.

For economy's sake in 1940, the New

Zealand Women's Institutes suggested a home-made sandsoap. This consisted of caustic soda, clean fat, resin, water, borax and 'half a kerosine tin of fine dry sand from beach'. This recipe required 15 minutes of boiling and stirring, and then a full month before the soap was ready for use. The truly patient housekeeper could then take the process one step further by producing some 'marvellous cleanser'. To grated sandsoap was added commercial washing powder and boiling water. Old floor-polish tins made ideal containers for the result.

With the arrival of electricity came new possibilities for cleanser manufacturers. Suitably charged were Warnock Bros and Taniwha Products who both produced Electric pumice soaps. The first worked 'in a flash' in 1937

Still to be found in homes in the older surburbs of our cities — and subject to regular polishing by Brasso — are examples of 'trench art': the Howitzer Shell Case Gladioli Vase, for example, and the Artillery Shell on Varnished Wooden Stand Doorstop. If it's not quite swords to ploughshares, these souvenirs of Anzac forays to the theatres of the Second World War took on a domestic burnish a long way from their original purpose.

As well as the shells — some of which lay around homes still armed — there were the muck-metal crocodiles, with moving jaws, made by Kiwi engineers serving in the North African campaigns. Brought home by returning servicemen who were, as Michael King has described in his history of the period, *After the War,* keen 'to build homes, raise children, grow vegetables and flowers, and holiday by the sea', these leftovers of war served as reminders of what it had taken to achieve the current state of grace.

while the other was simply 'the acme of sand-soaps'.

Another scientific milestone quickly noticed by the local soap industry was the discovery of X-rays by Wilhelm Röntgen in 1895. Within two years Norton & Co. of Wanganui had come up with X-Ray pumice soap, a versatile product that could scrub floors and double as a toilet soap. French scientist Marie Curie inspired the Radium Polish Company of Wellington in 1908. Like the radioactive element itself the manufacturers claimed of their floor polish that 'a little goes a long way', and also that their boot polish provided 'the shine of the times'. One can only wonder now whether the company was aware of the fact that Marie Curie herself was, by birth, Polish.

A cleanser of the 1920s that battled its way through to the '50s in a distinctive yellow tin was Clever Mary, 'the enemy of grease'. If this implied an element of feminine cunning then Old Dutch cleanser resorted only to old-fashioned Flemish thoroughness.

There is one company in particular that has been cleaning up New Zealand for over a century: Reckitt & Colman. With one notable exception, their range of scourers and polishes has been developed in Britain. Nevertheless, many became household names here as well, and none·more so than Brasso. This 'non-injurious' metal polish first came to New Zealand in 1907. Local production began in 1933 and it soon became particularly familiar to schoolboys buffing up their brassware for compulsory military drill.

The distinctive Brasso label survives today in a simplified form.

Brasso's famous stablemate Silvo first arrived to brighten up New Zealand's silver — not to mention electro-plate, pewter and chromium — in 1914. Both polishes are still made at Avondale in Auckland, but a third member of the family is no longer with us — a victim of kitchen technology. The striking yellow and black radiant Zebo tin promised an 'easy, quick, bright' polish for stoves, grates and ranges.

In a round flat tin came the more directly named Zebra. In 1912 this paste enamel stove polish cost 3½*d* per tin, and the blacklead version was 8*d* per dozen. Alternatively there was Whizz or, to put an early morning sparkle on the stove, Rising Sun blacklead.

Home and hosed

Despite the domination of Lever products, one local soap had lengthy service in our laundries. Although disadvantaged with a monster of a name, Taniwha's 'Big Golden Bar of Purity' was, appropriately, a gold medallist at the 1926 Dunedin International Exhibition. It lathered freely 'in any water, hot or cold'. And for the large laundry it was available in a case of 27 bars, for 34/6 in 1923. Originally it was manufactured by the Union Oil, Soap and Candle Co. of Albert Street, Auckland, but later moved out to Westfield, presumably to be close to the source of tallow. Later still, Taniwha went to Dunedin to be taken over by McLeod Brothers, also makers of Laundrine.

The Union Oil, Soap and Candle Co. produced a number of 'household favourites'. These included Jubilee wax and Britannia sperm candles which, like Taniwha, are now gone. However, there is a survivor: Sylvia starch, originally in a dark blue packet sporting a negro youth in a large white shirt. For obvious reasons this image had to go, and Sylvia is now a liquid in a plastic bottle, and made by Boots.

The Big Golden Bar of Purity.

Nineteenth-century European emigrants to New Zealand left behind an increasingly industrial landscape. Compared to 'dark satanic mills' and urban congestion, the countryside in the antipodes was, literally, a breath of fresh air. Fortunately the industrial revolution also brought improvements in more personal matters such as hygiene and sanitation. It was a true Victorian who claimed 'cleanliness is next to godliness', but to practise this maxim the new settler may have had little more than a handy stream for a laundry or bathroom. However, by the early 1880s the byproducts of a growing meat industry were already sustaining 15 soap and candle works.

Brett's *Colonists' Guide and Cyclopaedia of Useful Knowledge*

provided various soap recipes. The enterprising settler could 'slack in a firken three pounds of good quicklime' and, after much boiling and stirring, produce 'an excellent hard soap for family use'. Alternative methods used lye of leached ashes, potash and melted and clarified fat. An economical washing fluid could also be produced from sal-soda and unslaked lime, but ordinary soap was still required for soiled waistbands and collars.

Soap-making at home was encouraged for another half-century. In 1936 it was claimed that laundry soap from the grocer had doubled in price in just two years. However, the concerned housewife could take solace in 5 lb of fat and a two-shilling packet of Soapsave, 'the wonder soapmaker'. With a gallon of

water this combination produced 20 lb of 'finest household soap', and saved 10 shillings in the process. Even in 1950, household guides gave alternatives to commercial soaps. Fat was boiled, its scum scraped off, and caustic soda, resin and water were added. The whole lot was boiled in the multi-purpose kerosine tin with borax and after two or three days the result was 'a beautiful white soap'.

Today, doing the washing is an increasingly automatic affair, demanding less time and attention, and most certainly not the manufacture of one's own soap. It is a far cry from the time when Monday was unfailingly earmarked for this weekly ritual. As a matter of pride it was not uncommon for surreptitious preparation to begin on

In the days when white was the predominant colour of business shirts and blouses, just how white your whites were was a measure of washday ability. If you weren't content with the cleaning action of a hot soapy wash, there were a number of blueing agents available to finish off the job properly. Perhaps best known of these was Reckitt's blue. Packed into little cotton bags it was added to the final rinse. And, like a number of other products of the fifties, it was advertised by a catchy radio jingle that everybody knew:

> In the final rinse use Reckitt's —
> Wonderful ... Reckitt's ... Blue

The blue bags doubled as efficient window cleaners and as a salve for insect stings.

Sunday evening, thereby beating the neighbours to the clothesline on the day.

Barring the services of a maid there was no avoiding washday preparation, which could be laborious: sorting, mending, stain-removal, pre-rubbing on a washboard, pre-soaking and the making of starch. But most important was the readying of the device central to the whole operation — the copper. This boiler, encased in steel and pumice, began life in a shed detached from the house. The villa brought the copper in under the same roof, the washhouse being at the rear with ready access to woodshed and clothesline. Coppers and their attendant tubs — originally of solid kauri (Ideel) and later of reinforced concrete (Hume) — were still being installed in New Zealand laundries in the early 1950s. Since then appliance technology has reduced the whole washday mechanism down to cupboard size, and copper boilers are a thing of the past. Some live on, however, polished up and recycled, maybe as firewood baskets.

Whether the housewife did her own washing or had domestic assistance on Mondays, there is no doubt whose work it was. In 1920, Methven washing boilers were the 'boilers for women'. At the same time, Booth, Macdonald & Co. of Christchurch were pushing their Lilywhite washing machine, with patronising references to the housewife. Their manually operated revolving barrel cut out practically all the terrors of washing day. And an advertisement for the Hudson reinforced concrete boiler showed two satisfied customers conversing over the back fence. Each has her boiler fired up with results guaranteed, because 'The Name is on the Furnace Door'.

The boiling of white cottons and linens in the copper — for 20 minutes, with shredded soap — was unpleasant and steamy. The transfer to the tubs for rinsing in successively hot, cold, and blue water, was aided by wooden utensils such as the personalised Dolly and Peggy, made by the Dunedin Iron and Woodware Company. But even when the clothes were wrung out, perhaps on an Acme wringer (whose 1936 model had resilient rubber rollers that did not break buttons), and pegged out on the line, the job was not yet over. Wooden tubs needed to be cleaned with sandsoap, the

copper scoured with Clever Mary and even the willow clothes-basket could be in for a washing with warm soapy water.

Manufacturers have exploited various aspects of washday, beginning with Easy Monday, 'the great labour-saver' in the 1920s. In the same positive vein were Laborlite, in bar or packet, and No Rubbing Laundry Help. Acclaimed performers were Peerless and IXL, while Velvet, Soft, Swan and Joy were presumably easy on hands. Serious contenders were Rough Scrubber and Carbolic, but today we can't tell whether Monkey meant business or not.

Then, as now, the soap industry was overshadowed by one manufacturer — Lever Brothers. This monopoly began in 1884 when William Hesketh Lever of Lancashire registered the world's first-

ever brand name for soap — Sunlight. Demand for the yellow bars proved so great that within four years Lever built the world's largest soapworks — and a garden village to accommodate the workers. In 1892 Queen Victoria made Lever Bros her official soapmakers, and in 1900 Robert Falcon Scott carried Sunlight to Antarctica. Nevertheless the hapless explorer was unable to clean up by beating Amundsen to the Pole.

New Zealanders were able to benefit from the product in the late 1880s when it was imported from England and Australia. Then from 1919 it was made at Petone, a site personally selected by the now Sir William Lever. In 1924 it cost 7d per bar of two tabs. Today the world's oldest soap has diversified into squeeze-bottle dishwashing liquid.

The Lever legacy in New Zealand includes other household names such as Rinso and Lux. Production of these began at Petone's new flake mill in 1924. Rinso was heavily promoted nationally on Selwyn Toogood's radio quiz programmes in the '50s and '60s, but eventually fell victim to the automatic washing machine. In 1982 it disappeared from the market, in deference to its more modern stable-mate Persil. This product was born in Britain in 1907 and reached our shores about 1933. When dissolved it released a bleach, thereby rendering obsolete the familiar Reckitt's blue bag washing routine.

Early clotheslines were linear affairs, available in flax or heavily galvanised wire. The 1930s housewife was advised to dust the flax line before

The 'single steel tree' that graces many New Zealand backyards — the ubiquitous revolving clothesline — was a giant step ahead from the long wire line strung out from the house and lowered and lifted using a notched pole or paling. The first rotating line was the Australian Hills Hoist, originally designed and built by Lance Hill for his wife in the 1940s and later manufactured by him.

use, or to check the wire for rust. The 1950s saw the proliferation of the compact revolving variety, now a feature of every backyard. The popular all-steel Hills model of 1953 provided 103 feet of space and was complete with ball-bearings and locking pin.

The new washing machines did not convince everybody at first. The whole point of washday was, of course, to remove obvious dirt and deal with lurking germs. Housewives were continually implored to be ever vigilant for such hidden sources of disease and pestilence. In 1933 Old Dutch cleanser, for example, chased dirt (with a stick, according to the label) to provide a 'healthful cleanliness'. Ten years later some Luddites still considered the new washing machines less hygienic than the

traditional boiling-rubbing-scrubbing system. One wily advertiser therefore suggested the addition of a little Anti-Germ to the washing machine, to sterilise the clothes. Nevertheless, the method made possible by electricity did catch on, and housewives were urged to turn washing day into washing hour.

Thus such brand names as Beatty, Washrite, Speed Queen, Bendix and Whiteway entered the language and the laundries of New Zealand. These devices were, in essence, an agitator and bowl on legs — topped off with a wringer. The early 1950s models even displayed a modest form of streamlining, not unlike the automobiles of the day, a similarity further enhanced by the prominent gear stick on the side of the bowl. In 1961 Fisher & Paykel claimed their Whiteway

— the 'king of all electric washers' — meant 'less work for mother in over 200,000 New Zealand homes'. Now there was no scrubbing on the washboard, no heavy lifting of wet clothes and no old-style hand-wringing. But despite the genuine white porcelain enamel bowl with an anti-splash curve to the top rim, there could be drawbacks. After a bit of wear these four-legged appliances tended to exude oil on the laundry floor. Also, the exposed wringers were always a potential hazard for the operator, despite instantaneous safety release bars. Often the rubber rollers would fly apart when least expected. So there were few regrets when this generation of washing machines was eventually superseded by the square lines of the modern automatics.

Home and hosed

The distinction of being the country's oldest company with continuous grocery connections must go to L. D. Nathan. In the mid-1800s there was an extensive Nathan family in East London planning an assault on the antipodes. One non-emigrant was Uncle Henry, a successful clothing warehouseman, who plied the others with goods to start them off. Thus equipped, David Nathan arrived at the Bay of Islands via Sydney in 1840. It was at Kororareka, described at the time as the 'Hellhole of the Pacific', that Nathan set up shop. In rented premises on the waterfront adjoining Pompallier House the ambitious Sydney Commercial House was born. But these were uncertain times and, when it seemed that Auckland would become the new capital, Nathan smartly relocated —

southwards. Obviously he had an eye for business, as well as a supportive family. But there was also a strange coincidence: his father was Nathan Lion Nathan, perhaps a premonition of 1988 when the family firm would combine with New Zealand Breweries to form the giant Lion Nathan company.

From a tent on Auckland's waterfront, Nathan's Commercial House provided all the new settler's needs — from Wellington boots to powder flasks and groceries. His diversity knew no bounds, expecially in 1887 when the now prospering Nathans got into ostrich farming. The feathers were, briefly, the height of fashion, but this venture was ultimately a disaster. However, it did inspire the ostrich trademark which graced L. D. Nathan's popular Standard

(later, Roma) teas.

A typical New Zealand shopping basket would include Bell tea and Edmonds Baking Powder, household names that were given a great deal of exposure in the 1920s when implicated in debates over retail profits. A new name in economic shopping had just appeared — Self Help — and concerned competitors got together to combat the threat. They formed the Proprietary Articles Trade Association which, in essence, meant the fixing of higher profits. But Self Help stuck it out, in premises on Wellington's Lambton Quay. Within a year they had seven stores in the capital and, by 1931, had passed the hundred mark nationally. In 1933 they were up to 140, eventually to reach some 200. This might have been all good news

"Thank you for your custom!"

FOUR SQUARE

MR 4

The death-knell for many small general stores began ringing in the 1920s. There was unease about a new type of competition and small operators and their accumulated goodwill seemed about to be eliminated by the chainstore. This concern prompted the birth of what would later become the Four Square group. However, even with the new combined buying power, progress was slow for the new association. The breakthrough came in 1924 when the association became agents for a popular staple, the Te Aroha Diary Company's Arrow brand butter.

In the same year, while doodling on his calendar, the company secretary came up with a name for the group. His square around the date — the 4th — immediately struck home, and with an Archimedian 'I've got it' Four Square was born. To announce this, a hand-painted glass sign was provided for each store window.

By 1931 the company, now Foodstuffs Ltd, had 112 member stores and a corporate identity was called for. As a result the grocers took a field trip to Howick to check out the colour scheme of a Mr McInnes's store. This meeting presumably approved of the now familiar yellow and red livery. But the Four Square group had to wait another 20 years for its second famous identity, the smiling cartoon grocer with thumbs up and sharpened pencil at the ready. Appropriately, this character was the invention of the managing director, son of the originator of the Four Square symbol.

From then it was all growth: in 1950 'The Dominion's Largest Grocery Chain' boasted 700 stores, and in 1956 it acquired its 1000th member.

for the prudent shopper but there was a grubby side to the business. Because they could only obtain Edmonds Baking Powder on the manufacturer's terms, Self Help made their own. This they rather irreverently labelled Bound to Rise, which understandably inflamed the opposition. Edmonds were unsuccessful however, in seeking an injunction against the newcomer. And there was a twist to finish this tale. To compete with the cheaper Self Help product, the Maypole Stores group in Taranaki sought help — and got Acto — from Edmonds.

A feature of New Zealand's urban landscape is the considerable number of shops — high even by world standards. Nineteenth-century shops conformed to a general pattern. The verandahs, high wooden fronts and cluttered interiors had a boom-town quality. Particularly distinctive was the corner store, strategically placed to serve the community. Few of these 'general providers' have survived, with many now relieved of their enamelled signs and converted to residential use.

Until the 1950s the grocery store was an unhurried, dusty and aromatic place. The main physical features were the long, worn kauri counter almost hidden behind stacks of biscuit tins, and, from floor to ceiling, a bewildering array of goods on wooden shelves, accessible only by ladder. On the counter were the vital Avery scales and hand-cranked National cash register, the bacon slicer and a simple wire device for cutting cheese. There were also rolls of wrapping paper and, most likely, a sleeping resident cat,

Home and hosed

retained for mousing duties. Often, balls of twine and scissors were suspended from the ceiling for convenience.

Out the back, encroaching on the domestic quarters, were the barrels and bins from which bulk groceries were scooped and bagged. This was a job for Friday night after the customers had gone, or perhaps it provided pocket money for a young lad after school. Another important backroom duty in the days before pre-packaging was skinning the cloth off the 40 lb block of cheese. The more relaxed and personal nature of the business also allowed for telephone orders and home deliveries, the latter being effected by bicycle or perhaps by Bradford van.

By the late 1940s this style of grocery store was under threat. The rapid spread of the automobile and the demise of older inner-city areas was to be the ruin of the corner store. But there were other, external, influences at work. The future of the grocery trade in New Zealand was already apparent in North America, or the 'new world', so to speak. Major companies therefore despatched staff members on study tours for first-hand information. The first real benefit to the customer was the arrival of 'self-service', introduced to New Zealand by an Onehunga Four Square shop in 1948. In all fairness, however, the idea was not entirely new to this country. Eighteen years earlier the Farmers Trading Co. of Auckland had opened its own 'Help-Yourself Grocerteria' in its Hobson Street department store. Perhaps the name was a hindrance, but Farmers persisted. In

1952 they re-worked the concept and now called it the 'Self-Service Food Hall'. This presented perishables in the largest battery of food refrigerators in the country, as well as providing receipts detailing every purchase to the customer.

Self-service was a great leap forward for the grocery business. The long counter and high shelves were gone, and the shopper could now roam and select at will. Modern units displayed all of life's essentials, easily accessible and bathed in fluorescent light. The new system was greeted with enthusiasm by the grocers, with Four Square claiming over a hundred conversions in less than three years.

But many groceries were unable to take the next quantum leap. After 10 years of self-service in New Zealand

From small beginnings in mail-order supply, the firm of Laidlaw Leeds grew into the country's largest department store chain — Farmers Trading Company. Its founder, Robert Laidlaw, produced his first catalogue in 1910, the year after the opening of the North Island Main Trunk — a milestone in communication and the transport of goods, and a factor in the success of Laidlaw's fledgling venture.

The first catalogue — 118 pages, 5000 copies printed — offered a huge array of groceries, bedding, crockery, boots, hardware, saddlery and drapery. The legend on its cover — 'stern, old-fashioned, unfailing honesty' — and the company's adherence to a policy of 'the customer's always right' laid a solid foundation for the future. Catalogues continued to be issued up until 1938 (later ones were printed in lots of upwards of 70,000 copies) but long

before that time the company's direction had moved away from rural mail-order to city retailing.

In 1918 Laidlaw Leeds merged with the Farmers' Union Trading Company and by the early 1920s the first of the new department stores had been opened. The main branch in Auckland's Hobson Street was originally built by Laidlaw in 1914 as a warehouse. It is still the country's largest department store.

Farmers has always had a reputation for being at the forefront of service to customers. Their famous, free Auckland bus service began in 1922, escalators were installed in the Hobson Street store in 1955 and in 1957 shoppers could park at the city's first multi-storey carpark across the road from the store. The rooftop has been home to a children's playground since 1922.

Farmers rooftop playground.

another American idea arrived — the supermarket. This called for newer and larger premises, and names like New World and Foodtown, where prices could really be 'cut', 'slashed' and 'massacred'. The identity of New Zealand's very first supermarket depends on who's telling the story. Among the claimants is Foodtown at Otara. This establishment introduced South Aucklanders to self-opening doors, checkouts, a choice of 65 trundlers and, to make it all possible, 150 car-parking spaces in 1958. Alternatively, there was Four Square's man, Bill Miller, who opened his supermarket at Belmont, on Auckland's North Shore, about the same time.

The newer suburbs were served by the giant shopping centre, or mall, a complex of specialist shops with the

essential supermarket at its core. Lynmall was the country's first, in 1963.

Irrespective of where they are bought, New Zealand's grocery requirements remain fairly basic. In 1988 the 10 most popular items were, in order: Fernleaf butter, Home Style bread, Purex toilet rolls, Chef cat food, Chelsea white sugar, Anchor butter, Country Fresh eggs, Dairylea cheese, Winfield cigarettes and Tip Top bread. Further down the list were the national breakfast, Weet-Bix, a good all-rounder, Wattie's spaghetti, and a recent success story, Tegel frozen chicken. And, reflecting changing times, the top 20 also included Fresh 'n' Fruity yoghurt and Miracle margarine.

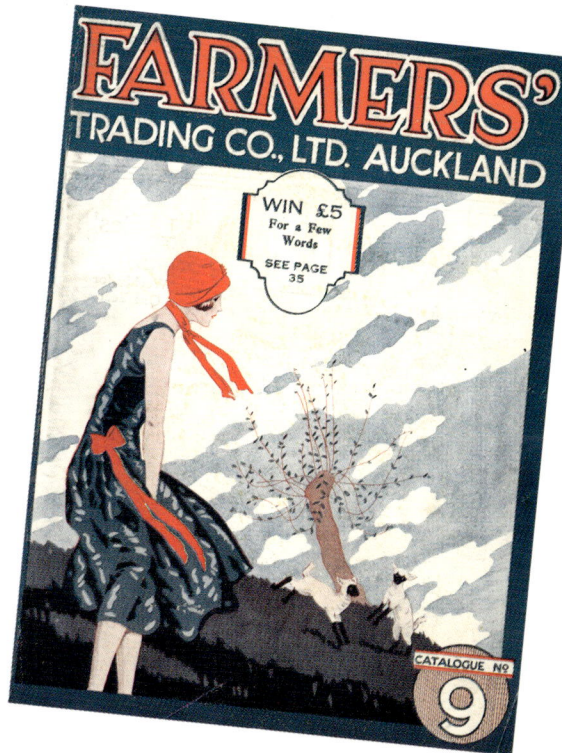

Home and hosed

New Zealanders have a voracious appetite for reading. But our book sales, among the world's highest per capita, suggest a more basic appetite. Of our twelve all-time best-sellers, no less than five have been concerned with cooking.

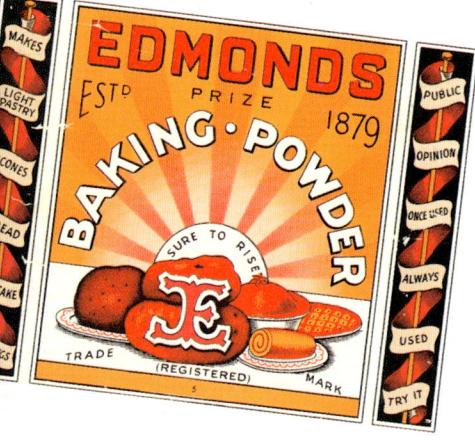

Perhaps as a consequence another two are on the subject of diet. But the *Edmonds Cookbook* reigns supreme: not only is it the country's best-selling book ever, but its total sales almost outnumber the New Zealanders themselves. Every home has one, or at least had one. But this national institution was only possible because of another — 'Sure to Rise' baking powder.

The first (1907) edition, a 50-page booklet, was a thinly disguised promotion for its most vital ingredient. However, it was free, initially, and to encourage good habits was regularly sent to engaged couples. It contained 'economical everyday recipes and cooking hints' in a regularly updated range of mealtime possibilities. In addition to

Cover of early Edmonds cookbook.

Albert Squares, Bath Buns and Sunbeam Cake there was, simply, Good Plain Cake and Mashed Potatoes. Alternatively, there was always Tripe, Suet Pudding or nine different varieties of scones.

WHILE Baking Powder will ever be a prosaic subject, still no New Zealander can learn of the great manufacturing achievement—the great commercial success—of Edmonds' "SURE TO RISE" BAKING POWDER without being proud of this great New Zealand Industry that has developed by sheer merit in the span of one man's life from the production of a few hundred tins to an annual production exceeding two million tins, and a circle of consumers that covers this Dominion and reaches as far afield as London.

'Sure To Rise', one of New Zealand's most durable, colourful and recognisable trademarks, had its origins in 1879. Twenty-year-old Englishman Thomas Edmonds arrived in Lyttelton and set up his own grocer's shop. But business proved sluggish and the enterprising Edmonds sought alternatives. Previous experience with sherbet convinced him to try baking powder. This decided, Edmonds then recognised that the most important feature of his new product would be its name. He even recorded for posterity the very incident that solved the problem. When asked by a disgruntled customer whether her scones would perform any better with this new baking powder, a confident Edmonds replied they were 'sure to rise'. Inspired by his claim he

then designed the distinctive rising-sun-with-cakes trademark.

A household name today it was no overnight sensation back in 1879. Although the historic first batch of 200 tins found a ready local market, the rest of Canterbury was oblivious to it. Edmonds therefore adopted a personal approach, taking free samples out into the province. He returned later to collect orders, and the rest is baking powder history.

Sure to Rise soon became a provincial and national favourite, with sky-rocketing sales. In 1912 the magic figure of one million tins per year was reached, and three years later sales were equivalent to six-and-a-half tins for every family in the Dominion. But it was not without competition. These other baking

powder compositions were also the subject of outrageous claims.

In 1905, for example, Sharland's Moa Brand proudly stressed that it contained no cream of tartar — whose residue was 'a hurtful drug'. By contrast, other powders (Edmonds included, presumably) were injuring the 'mental and physical health of thousands'. Perhaps unaware of these serious charges were such alternative brands as Kirkpatrick's 'K', Hamblin's 'Ideal', Ratjen's 'Grapeoid', Whitlock's 'Butterfly', Hall's 'King', Soppet's 'Diamond', Garland's 'Golden Gem', Hayward's 'Patty Pan' and Chrystall's 'Chef'. But perhaps much better known than most was Hudson's 'Balloon Brand', which claimed the largest sales in 'North New Zealand' in 1884. This variety sported fashionable

The Edmonds staff photographed in the factory gardens, 1932.

aeronautical imagery, with a balloon emblazoned 'Bound to Rise'.

Bound to Rise was up against Sure to Rise but it was the competitors' inability to guarantee success that encouraged Thomas Edmonds. And while other manufacturers offered a range of goods, Edmonds specialised in perfecting his powder. By 1928, when his sales hit the 2,500,000 mark, the competition must have been in tatters. Meanwhile, his baking powder became literally a prize product, with numerous awards at exhibitions of the day. Selected medals were proudly shown on an early label, beneath a plate of successful baking.

In addition to Hudson's, the 'Bound to Rise' boast was also made by the Self Help Co-op's own baking powder in the 1930s. To compete, Maypole Stores in

Home and hosed

Centrespread from the 1955 economy edition of the cookbook.

Thomas Edmonds gave New Zealand a lot more than just cooking ingredients and a book on how to use them. In 1929, to mark 50 years of business, he presented the city of Christchurch with a clock tower and a band rotunda. Both are still in existence, 60 years later, although the latter is now a restaurant — no doubt still benefiting from Edmonds products. During the Depression T. J. Edmonds Ltd was the first New Zealand company to introduce the five-day 40-hour week, achieving this with no redundancies. Another landmark was the construction, in 1922, of the Ferry Road factory, whose award-winning gardens have appeared on the cover of the cookery book since 1955.

Leavened baking relies upon a rising agent. The two most popular kinds in New Zealand are cream of tartar, the basis of Edmonds Sure to Rise, and a food phosphate, as used in Acto. ('Acto', as an abbreviation for the Australian Cream of Tartar Organisation, seems a curious choice for a product which contains no cream of tartar.) Both rising agents depend upon a chemical reaction. In the case of cream of tartar this is moisture-activated while Acto relies upon heat. The latter is therefore more often used by commercial bakeries as it enables the dough to be left standing for longer periods before cooking.

Taranaki sought help from Edmonds. They wanted a cheaper powder, and so 'Acto' was born, named after the Australian Cream of Tartar Organisation.

A worldwide shortage of cream of tartar a few years later pointed up the advantage of also producing an alternative rising agent. And it was a situation not helped locally by the loss of the steamer *Waikouiti* in 1941. Bound from Sydney to Lyttelton it was totally wrecked on Dog Island, near Bluff, with 130 tons of cream of tartar aboard. Fortunately Edmonds still had Acto to fill the gap, but it was 1946 before production of the flagship Sure to Rise brand was back to normal.

The turn of the century saw the arrival of a second product — custard powder, which was 'sure to please'. In the same vein were the very first Edmonds' jellies in 1936 — they were, logically 'sure to set'. They sure were, but somewhat prematurely. The early 'wet pack' varieties had a tendency to harden in the pack and be impossible to dissolve.

An entirely superficial change occured to Edmonds baking powder upon its centennial. Label regulations now required the product type to appear horizontally. Thus an enlarged 'Sure to Rise' replaced the old semi-circular 'Baking Powder', thereby preserving the spirit of Thomas Edmonds' original.

The cookbook, too, has not escaped changes. For a start is has been greatly enlarged, reflecting the increase in the range of the sponsor's products. But it has also moved with the times, incorporating gas cooking in 1971, metrication in 1976 and the microwave. However, despite constant updating, many recipes have survived unscathed from the orgininal edition.

Just as the famous cookbook stands alone as a national bestseller, so its progenitor, the baking powder, is unchallenged on grocery shelves. Once it had many competitors, but now it has none.

Home and hosed

'It must be Watties'

During James Wattie's lifetime his products carried his signature as a personal guarantee of quality. That his name had become a household one and his company, J. Wattie Canneries, one of the country's biggest, was due to his vision of a New Zealand self-sufficient in canned fruit and vegetables.

It was in the early 1930s, when the huge fruit and vegetable surplus of Hawke's Bay would each summer literally rot on the ground for want of a preserving facility, that James Wattie saw the opportunity for a local cannery.

It was a success from the very start and eventually the whole province felt the effect.

Directly and indirectly thousands of jobs were created in growing, canning and merchandising. From the bounty of the fertile Heretaunga Plains the province soon became known as the 'fruit bowl of New Zealand'. Some crops became of major commercial importance only because of the demand created by the canneries: peas, for example, were first grown for canning. Over the years, canned peaches, spaghetti, tomato sauce, baked beans, fruit salad, asparagus, as well as peas, came to be synonymous with the Wattie name.

Under James Wattie's direction, the situation that had existed in the early thirties, in which 80 percent of the country's canned food requirements were imported, was turned right around. In 1972, when Wattie retired, New Zealand was totally self-sufficient in fruit and vegetables and was a major exporter of these foodstuffs. As an indication of the importance the Wattie name had assumed, a university revue of the same period could include a song — sung to the tune of 'Land of Hope and Glory' — that went:

> Land of fern and paua,
> Nestled by the sea,
> Peaches, peas and baked beans,
> Canned by James Wattie!

As with most successful ventures, innovation has always been to the fore in the history of Watties. There was a continual pioneering of foods for canning and a pursuit of better, more efficient ways of doing the job. It was the first company to introduce quick-frozen foods to the New Zealand market in the late

One of the company's most memorable promotions was the 'It must be Wattie's' jingle. Written by Wattie's advertising agents, the first version featured ukelele accompaniment. Reduced these days to its exclamatory punchline, the complete jingle went:

> If it's rich in flavour and it
> suits the innerman,
> If it saves you money in your
> household plan,
> If it's nourishing and
> flourishing, goodness in the
> can,
> Then it's Wattie's,
> It must be Wattie's!

1940s. In the mid-fifties, prompted by a desire to use the fish waste from the company's fish-processing operations, Watties introduced prepared pet food. The first trademarks were Felix and Fido. And during the war years it was Watties that was responsible for production of the armed forces' basic diet — 'm & v', the canned meat and vegetable ration pack.

Today the Wattie name has ceased to exist as a single entity, rather it is a component of the New Zealand food giant Goodman Fielder Wattie. Sir James, Gisborne's most famous son, died in 1974.

On their way to your table — sliced peaches at the filling machine.

At first, the quick-freeze process froze peas in solid packs. As the competition in quick-frozen foods heated up James Wattie was keen to be the first to take the next step. He wanted free-flow peas and was determined to have them on the market for Christmas 1958. As happens, the first blast-freezing tunnel, necessary to produce free-flow products, was late being commissioned. So James Wattie had the peas frozen in a plate freezer in trays, then tipped on to a big stainless steel table where about a dozen people hit them with hammers and mallets — to produce instant free-flow peas.

On the Ball

On the ball

*G*eologically speaking, New Zealand is rugged, not to mention young and restless. Traditionally its citizens have felt much the same way — not that this is apparent under normal circumstances. Until recently weekends in our cities were internationally famous for their lack of action. The fact is, however, that the nation's energy, accumulated between Mondays and Fridays, finds its outlet elsewhere. And when the obligatory weekend chores of home-improvement and lawn-mowing have been disposed of, the people can turn to their real interests, which usually involve sport.

Over the years New Zealand has been promoted as a sportsman's paradise. Nowhere, it has been claimed, is the incentive to play in the open air greater than it is here. Not that weather has much to do with rugby — apart from having to decide between playing into, or with, the wind. No known meteorological phenomenon can interfere with this most venerated institution: rain, hail or shine, the game goes on.

Strictly speaking, sport is a form of recreation, a point lost on some New Zealanders. Nevertheless certain of our games have always been a serious business, for obvious and historical reasons. Wood-chopping, for example, was a regular feature of country sports days, alongside agricultural and highland dancing competitions. The sport fairly reflected the physical nature of the early farming days, when a livelihood was literally cut from the bush. And it is a wood-chopper from Tokoroa, Dave Lamberton, who has won the country's highest number of sporting titles ever — in excess of 70. Further, he has won championships (or 'chips') in Australia and Canada, and a number of world records as well.

Even today, when New Zealand cannot forget that it is small, distant and easily overlooked, at least there is still the sportsfield upon which we can make ourselves heard. Along with such diverse items as kiwifruit and jetboats, sport has contributed to the emergence of a sense of identity and national self-esteem.

More New Zealanders gather together in the name of sport than for any other reason. The country's largest ever spectator crowd numbered 65,000 and observed the 1959 Grand Prix at Ardmore. At races of a different nature

New Zealand's famous classic rugby jersey was developed by Lane Walker Rudkin. It was a tough, long-lasting garment which was taken up with gusto by rugby players and other sportsmen after its launch in the 1910s. Since the 1924 'Invincibles' team the jersey has been synonymous with All Blacks and in recent years, of course, the jersey has also achieved international status as leisure wear. Today's garment is made from a cotton-rich imported yarn and much effort has been spent in increasing the strength of the raw material and its ability to carry vivid colours — important when more than 300 different colour schemes are produced for rugby clubs in New Zealand alone.

Now known as Canterbury International, the company produces around half a million rugby jerseys each year at its Christchurch factory.

nearly 60,000 assembled to follow the Auckland Cup on Boxing Day, 1943.

Despite such serious interest in the subject, the New Zealand sports follower does not exhibit the hysteria associated with South Americans, for example. Compared to the expressive Latin soccer fan, the Kiwi rugby supporter is the strong silent type. Apart from sporadic barks of 'C'mon Black!' (or 'Blue!' or 'Gold!' etc.) or a helpful 'Spin it!' (or 'Ruck it!' or 'Nail 'em!'), the emphasis is rather on silent support. However, the desire to win is no less urgent or heartfelt, simply more restrained. In certain codes, players are now increasingly less inhibited about expressing their own feelings but the true rugby fan tends to provide support in much the same way as the forward goes about his game: relentlessly and with a certain lack of flair. The main difference is that the spectator, hemmed in on the bank, does not have the same opportunities to exhibit complete disregard for personal safety.

Although sport is a national preoccupation it is now an activity attracting fewer participants. New Zealand would hardly be alone in having television-watching as its most popular free-time activity, with reading second. It would be of little consolation to anyone concerned with the nation's physical fitness to realise that much televiewing and reading is on the subject of sport. And the armchair sports enthusiast is well catered for in this country, as the non-sporting viewer can testify.

Despite a body blow to its image resulting from the 1981 Springbok tour, New Zealand rugby has reasserted itself as our national game — a status it will probably never lose. Once the very antithesis of image-consciousness, the game's administrators have had to grapple with massive changes in recent years.

Moving with the times the traditionally clean-shaven macho rugby ranks have had to accept long hair, moustaches and beards. And to keep up with the play Auckland rugby now employs an administrator who was once an aspiring bleached-haired pop singer from New Plymouth — Lew Pryme.

Nowadays rugby claims by far the largest registered membership of any national sporting association — about

On the ball

The discipline! The uniforms! The precision! *Marching!* More than half a century after its emergence on the national scene, marching — part sport, part performance art — continues to enjoy a special place in our popular culture. Dating from the eary years of the Depression — the Auckland YWCA fielded a team in 1931 which gave demonstrations at charity events — marching is a New Zealand phenomenon despite its borrowing from American college drum majorettes.

Following the appearance of the YWCA team at 'cheer-up' rallies and fund-raising functions the Wellington Interhouse Marching Recreational Association was formed, which saw the setting up of

businesshouse teams and competitions, initially in both marching and athletics. The sport's popularity soon spread. The New Zealand Marching Association was founded in 1945, by which time the sport's connection with business houses had disappeared. Free from a 'house' uniform, teams now looked to the services for inspiration with their attire.

In its heyday in the 1950s, hundreds of teams of Midgets, Juniors and Seniors were going through their drills on sports fields and competing in regional and national competitions. The emphasis on team discipline, appearance and military-style uniforms appealed to a society which, three decades later, in more individualistic times, now

looks somewhat askance at the same things. And the attraction of other leisure activities has seen both declining numbers and an increasing average age.

But time has also seen a shift away from grim-countenanced marching girls following rigid routines. Today's teams — most usually seen by the public in parades and as warm-up acts for sporting fixtures — give more interesting, varied performances. *Eyes right!*

The Remuera Guards, 1960.

200,000. Second with 135,000 is bowls, comprising women's, men's and indoor, followed by netball with 114,000. Thereafter, in order, are football (or soccer) whose combined men's and women's total just edges out (men's) cricket, gymnastics, tennis, squash and yachting.

If rugby sometimes appears unruly to the uninitiated, it is certainly not a recent development. The country's first 'game' involved pupils of Christ's College, Christchurch, with a huge number of participants on a paddock. At the centre of it all was an inflated bullock bladder and an unusual set of rules. But New Zealand rugby as we now know it had its origins in Nelson in 1870 in our first club match, between Nelson College and 'The Town'. The same significant year saw our

first 'international' when sailors from HMS *Rosario* took on a team from Wellington. However, it was 1882 before the first real international opposition came to these shores, from New South Wales, with the first New Zealand team making the return visit two years later.

Rugby is a national subculture of immense proportions. At the very bottom of the ladder are the midgets and lowest grades, characterised by their lightness and bare feet. Schoolboys once hauled extra shorts over their good pants for earnest matches during precious lunchtimes and breaks — a bit restrictive on movement but a welcome saving on washing. If the vital ball, or 'pill', was misplaced or commandeered by others, a

game of bullrush was probably substituted.

Official team practice was usually after school, assuming a sympathetic teacher could be talked into coaching. The all-important match was either Wednesday afternoon or Saturday morning. Senior boys had the comparative luxury of a sleep-in, with their fixtures perhaps on Saturday afternoon.

When schooldays were over allegience was transferred to a local club, often the high school 'old boys'. Even if this did not prove the stepping stone to provincial representation or All Black-hood it did guarantee camaraderie and after-match functions for life. And if one were fortunate enough to make it right to the top and wear the silver fern, life would never be the same again. To

General Motors Marching Team, 1930s.

become one of the chosen few is to gain a certain aura, and perhaps the closest thing this country has to a life peerage. The family name assumes an extra dimension, and the All Black himself will soon be addressing assembly halls of eager young players. Further, he might be approached to endorse the local car dealer's merchandise, or perhaps be offered a job by a tobacco or beer company.

In some schools rugby assumed the role of a fourth 'R', being treated as an extremely serious business somehow central to school spirit and the business of character-building. This was most evident when some of the older schools met their annual arch-rivals. New Plymouth Boys' High, for example, had such an arrangement with St Pat's,

Silverstream, resulting in an annual clash at a neutral halfway point, usually Hawera in South Taranaki. On one occasion when NZ Railways supplied transport for the northern contingent, boisterous supporters inflicted considerable damage to the train — thereby pre-dating soccer hooliganism by a number of years. The incident had major repercussions at the next morning assembly: the headmaster, with able assistants, caned the whole school. In fairness to the NPBHS, most schools can probably recall more than a few similar colourful rugby anecdotes.

The oldest rugby rivalry in the country is jointly claimed by Otago Boys' High and Christ's College. Unfortunately there were years when the tradition lapsed, and so the oldest uninterrupted

record really belongs to the Boys' Highs of Waitaki and Timaru. Their rivalry dates back to 1884 and survived even the odd epidemic. On these occasions both schools had to resort to teams of inferior quality in order to preserve the tradition. In spite of what pestilence may have been passed around in the scrum, the rector of Timaru Boys' maintains that these games 'greatly enhanced the traditons of both schools and . . . proved the source of many enduring personal friendships'.

It is at the provincial level that our rugby rivalry is most earnest, particularly if the Ranfurly Shield is at stake. The 'Log o' Wood' has been fought over since 1902, and monopolised mainly by Auckland, Canterbury and Hawke's Bay. Holding the shield for a length of

On the ball

Life is seen by the cricket cognescenti as a metaphor for cricket — the winning or losing of no great concern, but rather that life should be played well. As in cricket, you may face the occasional bouncer or risk being caught out in the deep, but each day, like each delivery, provides a chance to play on. For some the game has the appeal of a religion. . .and may enjoy certain similarities.

At Christ's College, Christchurch, it was not uncommon in years gone by (it may still occur today) for pairs of schoolboys in chapel congregations to while away the tedium of services by playing a form of cricket. The usual rules were followed with each boy representing a team for the

Boundary 6.

Boundary 4.

Out.

duration of a ten-wicket two-innings test. Settled in their pews they would then await the scoring as signalled by the umpire, a role played unwittingly by the minister. A particularly expressive man of the cloth would naturally have the game moving along at a fair clip, while the more restrained padre would place the getting of a result in the time available somewhat at risk.

time ensures a 'golden age' for the local union, usually resulting in a new grandstand or two. Another benefit was being let out of school early for a mid-week challenge, if one had a supportive headmaster. Traditional rivals made a real parade of it, with floats, bands, clowns on funny bikes, and the inevitable marching girls down the main street prior to a Saturday challenge. Team mascots, such as Waikato's 'Mooloo' and Taranaki's 'Ferdinand', added to the festivities.

Rugby is hardly everyone's cup of tea. But it is, almost, a way of life for many and an unavoidable feature of our landscape. Its goalposts, like the distinctive architecture of our ubiquitous racing clubs, are everywhere: totems to a nation of 'sports'.

'Not rain, nor sleet, nor dark of night. . .'

Given the importance the country attaches to horse racing — more than $1 billion plunged by punters each year — it was not surprising that New Zealand was the first country to install a totalisator. Invented by an Australian, George Julius, the 'tote', as it is known, is an electromechanical wonder that makes the complex mathematical calculations required at race meetings. Representing one of the very earliest on-line, real-time computers, the totalisator replaced the small armies of clerks previously required to work the *pari mutual* betting system that is used on racetracks.

Devised by the French in the 1860s, the *pari mutual* system has the bets on the various runners in a race accumulating into a pool in which the bettors backing the winners share, in proportion to the size of their bet. The distribution of the bets placed on

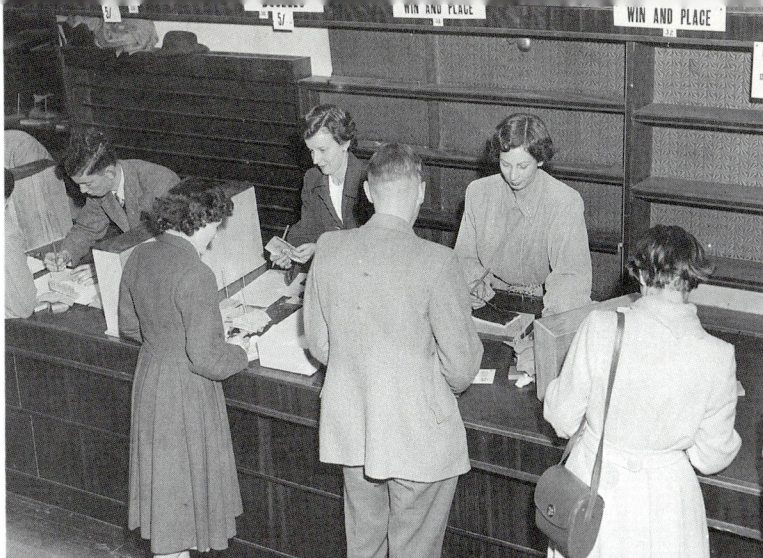

the horses results in the odds against the horse winning. Thus the odds change continuously as betting progresses, until the start of a race — the odds that apply then are those paid out on.

In comparison bookmakers give fixed odds at the time the bet is made, and these do not alter. If the bookie offers bad odds then he or she may be out of pocket if their total takings are insufficient to cover the

winning payout. Not so with the tote, where the size of the pool is a factor in calculating the winning dividends. The tote never loses.

The world's first tote opened at Ellerslie racecourse in 1913 and in 1921 bookmaking was made illegal. In 1951 the Totaliser Agency Board — the TAB — opened betting shops to provide Kiwis with the option of off-course betting.

The Ellerslie tote, 1925.

On the ball

The success of Arthur Lydiard's runners, Snell especially, created for youngsters an atmosphere of enticing possibility. If it didn't work out on the All Black front, then, no problem, you were odds-on for setting the next mile record. Snell was strong, fast and, typical of New Zealanders at that time, humble with it. The Lydiard training methods, coupled with Snell's talent, produced a stamina that meant he could go through three-and-a-half laps or more at pace and then still have the power to kick home in a sprint.

The excitement of his smashing the mile record at Wanganui in 1964 won't have been forgotten by anyone conscious at the time.

'Round-the-Bays', Auckland.

Joggers are undoubtedly members of the country's biggest mass movement (the annual Auckland Round-the-Bays jog is normally run by upwards of 70,000 people) and recognition for putting this country on its feet, literally, must go in the main to one man ... Arthur Lydiard.

The popularity of jogging in New Zealand — indeed, arguably, its popularisation internationally — grew out of encouraging postwar attitudes to health and recreation as part of social development coupled with the focus on running provided by the tremendous success of New Zealand runners at the Rome Olympics of 1960 and again in Tokyo four years later. These track successes were a direct result of Lydiard's training system which emphasised strength and stamina.

The first jogging club was formed in Auckland in 1962 by Colin Kay and Arthur Lydiard and within a few short years the deeds of the great middle-distance runners, Peter Snell, Murray Halberg, Barry Magee, Bill Baillie and Ray Puckett, had influenced thousands of less extraordinary Kiwis to don training shoes and take to the parks and footpaths. Jogging became part of our national life.

Arthur Lydiard's legacy is today's joggers who, singly or in groups, are a common feature of the suburban scene — enjoying the rewards of fitness and good health that sustained aerobic exercise brings.

Peter Snell.

New Zealanders can only speculate on how they might have managed without their frozen meat export trade. The successful arrival of the *Dunedin's* cargo in London in 1882 ensured that New Zealand would never be the same again. But had this enterprise failed, New Zealand would have survived, somehow. Already it was an energetic manufacturer, quick to exploit its rich resources.

In 1881, for example, the nation's farmers were providing sufficient raw material for 40 boiling-down and meat-preserving works. Byproducts from these supplied 17 bone-cutting mills and 15 soap and candle works. There were also no less than 119 fellmongering, woolscouring and tanning works, the latter fuelling another 31 boot factories.

In all there were nearly 1500 such establishments, from flax mills and rope works to gold mines and potteries. All this activity ensured a national thirst, and encouraged a further industry. In 1881 just over half a million New Zealanders supported 79 aerated water factories and 99 breweries.

Local brewing hardly got off to an auspicious start. Captain Cook's 1773 recipe, requiring rimu leaves and ship's molasses, is best left in the archives. Nevertheless, Cook did receive a rare and posthumous honour — a brewery in his name in Khyber Pass, Auckland. Today it is gone, absorbed by a national giant, but a statue of its mentor remains.

The Captain Cook provided a popular brew in the 1940s: the drink of the day was the Brewery's Imperial ale, more

generally known as the Brown Bomber. Whether this was in recognition of the current world heavyweight champion, Joe Louis, because, like him, it packed a punch, is not recorded. However, such was the popularity of the nickname that the manufacturers changed their label accordingly. But this new look didn't catch on, and the beer disappeared altogether.

The story of beer in New Zealand is nothing if not colourful. As a true and proper drink of Englishmen it was, like tea, bound to catch on. Along the way the national beverage has reflected the country's history, and created much of its own. The colonial climate and the outdoor lifestyle ensured a thirst for a few 'cold ones' and the early days of European settlement were noted for the

proliferation of local breweries. Work may well be the curse of the drinking class, but the breweries have relentlessly pursued the working man. This was never more apparent than when gold fever struck: Thames was once congenial host to not less than 80 hotels. These establishments — hotel being too kind a term for most — were replenished by a plethora of breweries. Nationally the figure reached 102 in 1890, but centralisation soon took hold. Eventually two giant empires emerged and local labels were absorbed as national brands penetrated the provinces.

If the British introduced the taste for beer to New Zealand, the Germans obliged with the technology. Joseph Kuhtze of Munich ran away to sea, only to be shipwrecked near Dunedin. By

1860 he was carrying on the family brewing tradition near Cromwell, and later at Hawke's Bay and Palmerston North. Following generations of anglicised 'Coutts' were, predictably, also brewers. Son William owned the Main Trunk Brewery in Taihape, and later established the Waitemata Brewery, the beginnings of the mighty DB group.

A third generation Coutts, Morton, had exhibited Kiwi ingenuity at an early age: his invention of continuous fermentation in the 1950s was a world first. The Coutts method superseded the old open-vat system, and produced a better product and in larger quantities. To show its appreciation of the new process New Zealand, in 1960, became the third-biggest beer-drinking population in the world. And now that it

is safe to be German again, the original Kuhtze family name has been reinstated, on a modern lager.

From Hamburg came another German brewer, Louis Ehrenfried. He set up business in Thames and successfully slaked the thirsts of the goldminers. Through amalgamation in 1897 Campbell and Ehrenfried was born. Nineteen years later this Auckland brewery absorbed the Great Northern of Khyber Pass, a company which had used a lion on its label since at least 1885. This beast provided the identity for the new brewery. Then in 1923 came the final step, when eight others from around the country joined up to become New Zealand Breweries.

Not so welcome in New Zealand was Otto von Bismarck, Chancellor of Prussia

and architect of modern Germany. In 1889 he appeared on this country's first lager beer, bottled by the Captain Cook Brewery. As the First World War approached, things Germanic became decidedly undesirable and Bismarck faded from the scene.

Continuing the German brewing tradition on the local market is Steinlager, NZB's finest achievement, and not bashful about its international success. This award-winner began life in 1958 when the 'Black Budget' of that year restricted, among other things, the import into New Zealand of such luxury goods as continental-type lagers. To fill the vacuum New Zealand Breweries responded with a batch-brewed lager called Steinecker. Its early success in the American market attracted the attention of Dutch brewer Heinecken who felt the upstart's name was too close to their own and forced a name change.

When Captain Cook concocted his landmark, but vile, brew, he was not catering for a shipload of drunken sailors. It was the prevention of scurvy that he had in mind, and so local brewing got off to a health-conscious start. Other early visitors in need of a drink had to bring their own, and some extremely potent and suspect beverages reached these shores. As a form of quality control, the truly public-spirited Joel Polack set up New Zealand's first brewery, at Kororareka, in 1835. Ominously, it also had the distinction of being the first European industry established in New Zealand.

Subsequent brewers were quick to

On the ball

New Zealanders' first exposure to restaurant wine was concentrated on two wines in particular, both carrying the McWilliams label.

The first of these, a red, was the notorious Bakano which became a household name throughout New Zealand from the mid 1950s. Beginning with the 1954 vintage, the original Bakano — a blend of hybrid and vinifera grapes — enjoyed immense popularity among those who wanted a 'classical style' red wine at a modest price. The success of this wine was further enhanced by its selection for use by the French rugby team when it toured this country in 1968. In fact, the result was a severe shortage of the 1964 vintage which had already been on strict allocation. Bakano was also selected by Air New Zealand (TEAL as it was then) as the first New Zealand table wine to be served in flight.

All grapes used to produce Bakano came from Hawke's Bay vineyards, from its first bottling until the original blend was discontinued with the 1983 vintage. Today Bakano has been re-launched as a blend of New Zealand and Australian cabernet sauvignon.

Cresta Doré was another from the McWilliams stable that became synonymous with dining out in the 1960s and 1970s. First released as a 1954 vintage, Cresta Doré was then made from a blend of white wine grapes. However, from 1970, muller thurgau grapes alone were used to produce the elegant and fruity style that it became famous for. And one stage its popularity meant that it too had to be rationed to wholesalers to ensure a fair distribution. Cresta Doré was discontinued in 1984.

push the health-giving benefits of their beers. DB ales, for example, were variously described as 'healthful', 'a nourishing tonic' and 'rich in vitality'. Tonic was indeed the key, with beer even being prescribed by doctors to ease tension and aid digestion. The breweries' interest in health extends these days to the sportsfield. Mud-splattered rugby players therefore peer from hoardings, proclaiming the invincibility of DB Brown. In response, Lion Red is 'a measure of a man's thirst'. Other brands have sailed on ambitious yachting challenges. In all these campaigns the wily public cannot be fooled: the breweries may be promoting sport, but they are really advertising beer.

For sportsman and armchair enthusiast alike, the after-match function is a necessary post-mortem. Both can be grateful that prohibition is a distant memory, but in 1919 it nearly carried the day. Only the votes of the soldiers overseas ensured New Zealand's continuance. But there was one concession — a temporary war-time measure — that became a national institution. Few aspects of New Zealand life have amazed, or appalled, foreigners quite as much as six o'clock closing. This ritual involved the consumption of as much beer as was physically possible in the hour after work. Until its abolition in 1967 it was standing-room only. Public bars were designed only for efficient mass drinking and, afterwards, easy cleaning. These male preserves also bred other habits, in particular the practice of 'shouting'. This fairly distributed the

I VOTE FOR CLOSING AT 6 P.M.

~~I VOTE FOR CLOSING AT 10 P.M.~~

The 'six o'clock swill' identified that hour or so between the end of the working day and the closing of hotel bars prior to 1967. While the law was designed to encourage family life in the home the result was often a piggish, drunken binge where the incentive was to knock back as much booze as possible as quickly as possible. Writer David McGill has described the situation as 'the closest we got to a direct connection between beer hoses and the customer'. In fact it was the jug that was the vessel dearest to the serious drinker's heart, obviating as it did time-consuming queueing for 'schooners', time which could be better spent in putting it away.

Even the lowly bottle-top has been the subject of contemplation. Legends tell of hardy types removing them with their navels — a task now made easier by the new twist-tops. A much safer party trick is to open one's bottle with a deft flick of another. And afterwards the discarded tops can be put to good use — as a boot-scraper for the back porch.

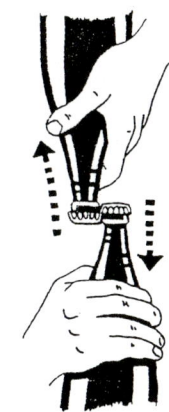

Step 1.

Step 2.

responsibility, and cost, of a continuous supply of drinks. Time was when even the publican would assist, by providing every third or fourth round 'on the house'.

Pubs have long provided for community identity. Students, for example, have traditionally favoured particular local hostelries such as the (late) Kiwi in Auckland, the Duke in Wellington and the Captain Cook in Dunedin.

In the pub and bottle-store there have been many changes. Jugs are now plastic and cans supplement bottles. Originally of tin but now aluminium, the shrink-wrapped six-pack has given beer a new portability. As a result the flagon, or half-gallon jar — the serious drinker's weekend backstop — has all but disappeared. And to carry it all, the dozen crate and carton were developed. For whatever function, bringing your own is facilitated by drive-in bottle-stores and strategically placed outlets. Party-goers were once required to BYOG, but even this has been abbreviated — the Grog now taken for granted.

On the ball

Clear & Refreshing as a Mountain Stream

LEMON AND PAEROA NATURAL MINERAL WATER

The Highest Achievement of the AERATED WATER BOTTLERS ART

L&P

Over the years the packaging of Lemon & Paeroa has changed as often as the identity of its owners. But one element has remained central throughout, the essential lemon. An anatomically correct profile of the fruit once dominated the label, with the drink's name spelt in full. But as the lemon evolved into an oval, the name became simply L&P. This abbreviation acknowledged common usage, and also eliminated a bit of a tongue-twister for non-New Zealanders.

American culture has always found a ready market in New Zealand. Despite our traditional English ties we have kept one eye on developments on the furthest shores of the Pacific. In the 19th century we shared a free trade in goldminers, bringing, among other things, Levi Strauss jeans to this country. The American building industry took our kauri, and when that had run out we took their oregon. Then, after the First World War the Californian bungalow arrived via Australia to become the national home.

During the next war we were hosts to American servicemen and a further up-date of their culture. While these GIs didn't exactly introduce coffee or chewing gum, for example, they did raise our awareness of things American.

The most successful US export has been Coca-Cola. Intriguingly, when this beverage first appeared in Atlanta, Georgia — in 1886 — it is possible that New Zealand had just invented its own classic drink.

High achievers often have humble origins, and Lemon & Paeroa is no exception. It began in a cow paddock where Paeroa residents discovered a spring that provided a refreshing drink. Some folk, well ahead of their time, were even given to adding a slice or two of lemon to the water for flavour. Then, inevitably, big business got in on the act and the Paeroa Natural Mineral Water Company began a bottling operation.

At first the beverage was seen more as a therapy than a thirst-quencher, a popular attitude supported by the government balneologist in 1904. Dr Arthur E. Wollman's official analysis described the 'mild alkaline akalybeate water containing a somewhat large proportion of magnesium carbonate' as valuable for medicinal purposes … but not much else. He saw it as a table water but wasn't sure anyone would go to the expense of bottling it. Such was the consumption of tea in New Zealand in 1904 that Wollman saw no future for any alternative drink.

Nevertheless, in 1907 Menzies & Co., who already had aerated cordial factories at Te Aroha, Waihi, Hamilton and Thames, took the plunge and purchased the Paeroa company. At first the new owners simply packaged the natural water, but soon, no doubt on local advice, began adding lemon. The

COMPOUND CORDIAL

PEPPERMINT

B B
NO ONE CAN PASS US

BALLINS INDUSTRIES LTD.,
9 BYRON STREET
CHRISTCHURCH
CONTAINS PRESERVATIVE

Aerated Beverage PRESERVATISED
FLAVOURED
SWEET ORANGE
ARTIFICIALLY COLOURED
MARLBOROUGH
BREWERY CO LTD
·BLENHEIM·

ARTIFICIAL BEVERAGE
COCKTAIL SPECIAL
The MARLBOROUGH
BREWERY CO. LTD.
GROVE ROAD, BLENHEIM
CONTAINS PRESERVATIVE

What Schlitz beer has done for Milwaukee, a soft-drink is still doing for Paeroa. In recognition, there stands at the intersection of State Highways 2 and 26 the town's most famous feature, and possibly the biggest 'bottle' in the world. The bottle is a 7-metre tall monument to the nation's most durable home-grown soft-drink, 'the highest achievement of the mineral bottler's art'.

company merged to become Grey & Menzies and in 1909 was shipping wooden casks of the water to its Auckland factory. There it was flavoured and bottled for distribution to an expanding market.

Obviously, transporting natural mineral water to Auckland, or anywhere, would make for an expensive beverage. Fortunately there was a better way, inspired by an early general manager. Thus water from the original bore was analysed and dispensed as 'A.G.M. salts', named for Mr Allan G. Menzies. The product could then be made anywhere — it was simply a matter of adding pure water to these vital salts. The confident manufacturers claim the result is indistinguishable from the real thing. But regulations do not permit

misrepresentation and so modern labels read 'sparkling' — as opposed to 'natural' — mineral water.

By the early 1960s the majority of the country's hotels were owned by the two large breweries, Dominion and New Zealand. But L. D. Nathan Ltd also had hotels and, to ensure a supply of their life-blood, bought a brewery of their own, the Waikato Brewery. This had been owned by C. L. Innes Ltd. The latter had merged with L&P's bottlers Grey and Menzies in 1963 to form Innes Tartan Ltd.

The 1964 sale of Innes to Nathan's gave L&P international stable–mates in Coca-Cola and Schweppes and Nathan's established the giant Oasis bottling complex at Mt Wellington in Auckland to manufacture the trio of soft-drinks. The story is a familiar one — the

centralisation of industry. Whereas small bottlers had once catered to local demands, monopolies now dictated. Big rigs could deliver Oasis products deep into the heartland, displacing local filling lines. Fanta, for example, was introduced to New Zealand by Pike and Waters Ltd of New Plymouth about 1960, an event marked by the distribution of a truck-load of free samples around Mt Egmont. Nowadays, all Taranaki's soft drinks are trucked in from Auckland.

There is, of course, no disputing the nation's favourite soft-drink. Nevertheless, while Coke continues to top the sales charts, Lemon & Paeroa accounts for 6 percent of the market, well over 8 million bottles per year.

On the ball

Tobacco came to New Zealand with the first Europeans, who probably lit up as soon as they were ashore.

The Maori people were ready converts to tobacco and grew it for their own use. Indeed they were encouraged to do so with *The Culture of the Tobacco Plant* translated into Maori in 1867 by order of His Excellency Sir George Grey, 'for the information of the Maori race'. The habit was an old one: the Maori had traded for clay pipes with some of their first European vistors. Rediscovered in excavations, these pipes now enable us to date these early contacts. The most romantic images of the Maori use of tobacco came from the brush of Charles F. Goldie, from about 1906 to 1938. With such titles as 'Memories', 'The Anxious Moment — The Last Match' and 'Kapai!

Te Toriri!' ('Good! The Tobacco!'), the nostalgic portraits recorded elderly Maori men and women with moko and pipe.

New Zealand's suitability for growing tobacco was quickly recognised. The North Auckland region was found ideal for Virginia leaf, Taranaki for cigar tobacco, and even Queenstown measured up. In the 1880s a Tauranga grower successfully cropped four types of leaf which he identified as 'Turkish, Virginian for cake tobaccos, Virginian for cigar wraps and native or Maori Leaf'.

But not all our early local leaf ended up in pipes or cigarettes — some was destined for the sheep-dip. 'Black Leaf 40', available through the 1930s, was named for its 40 percent content of nicotine sulphate. Apart from guarding against lice, tick and scab in sheep, it

was also handy in the garden and poultry yard.

The importation of smokers' requisites has always been a lucrative business — especially for the government. In the late 19th century local growers could have easily supplied the national need but were discouraged by draconian legislation. Nevertheless, in 1884 local growers produced 4776 lb of tobacco, and the following year the Auckland Tobacco Company proudly showed the results at the Industrial Exhibition in Wellington. Interestingly, their cigars were 'appropriately named with Maori appellations'. However, their products were far from all New Zealand-made. Their best cigars, in fact, were one-quarter colonial leaf and three-quarters American. Perhaps local leaf

The National Tobacco Company's most durable smoke proved to be 'Riverhead'. In 1945 this product claimed it was 'the smoke that made New Zealand famous', although it probably did more for one or two individuals than it did for the country. Originally, National Tobacco's products came in small 2 oz tins and 1 lb and 3 lb cannisters, but in 1938 a new package appeared — the flat tin or 'pocket edition'. Two years later, wartime restrictions led to the change to a cardboard packet. It is in this form that Riverhead Gold, now re-named Pocket Edition, lives on today.

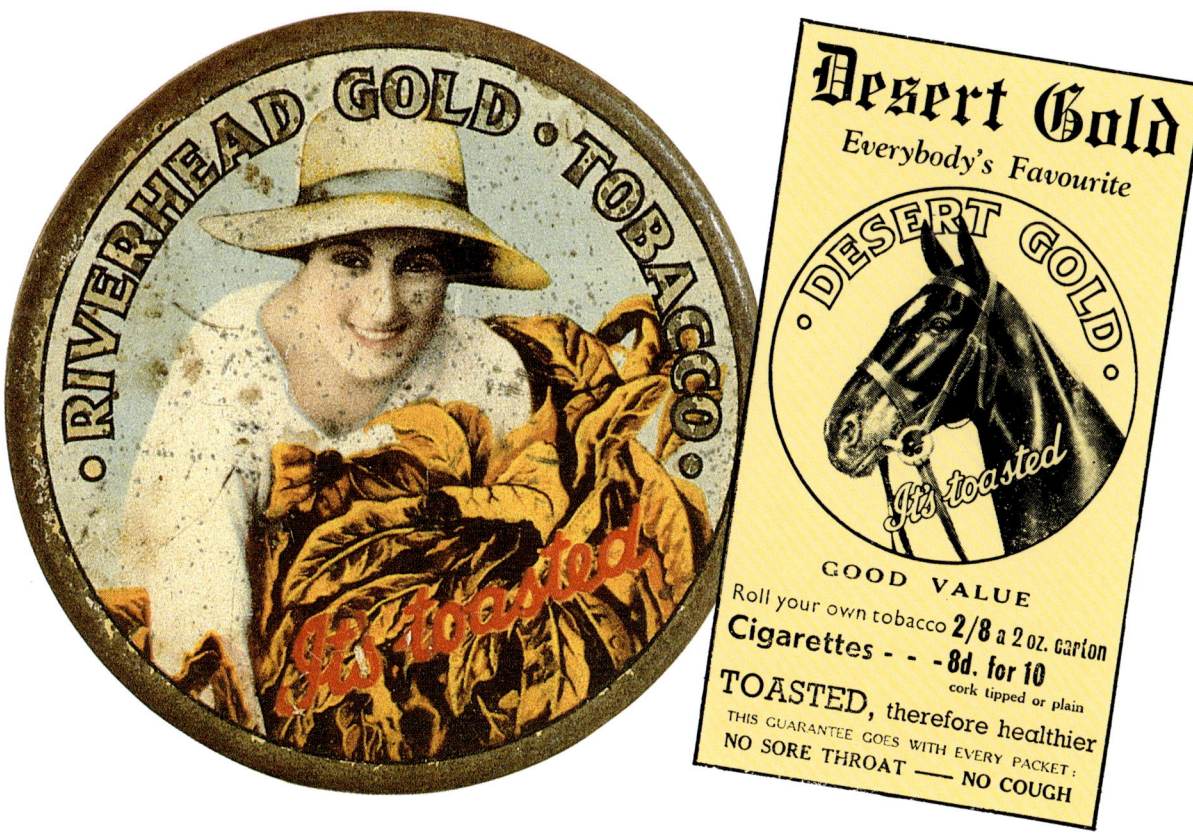

was still only good enough for the sheep-dip.

The Auckland area perhaps saw the birth of the New Zealand tobacco industry. In the 1870s one E. W. Gotch was growing five acres at Papakura, as were A. Brown & Sons nearby in Tuakau. Then there was the extensive New Zealand Tobacco Manufacturing Co. which was filling 5000 cigars per day in 1886. It had agreements with 113 growers throughout the country, supplying them with free seed and instruction in return for leaf. In the 1890s one Austin Walsh produced 'Long Cut Auckland Gems' cigarettes at his own Atlas Bonded Factory.

Meanwhile, in Europe, Gerhard Husheer was learning the business. In 1921 he emigrated from Germany to

become involved with a tobacco company in Napier, New Zealand. Next he directed his attentions to the old Riverhead gumfields near Auckland and formed a tobacco syndicate with two well-known merchants — Enoch Bond (of Bond & Bond) and John Burns. Later he began the National Tobacco Company, whose success attracted other companies to the district. The boom didn't last, with many smaller operations surviving by amalgamating. Husheer came out on top and bought the Napier factory he had once been associated with. His 200 acres at Riverhead had struck 'gold' and were to supply some of the country's household names in tobacco.

By the mid 1930s the National Tobacco Company had a range of five products. There was the Navy Cut No. 3,

whose label of a pipe-smoking bulldog, despite his studded collar, claimed 'no bite'. For a rural flavour there was Cut Plug No. 10, known as 'bullshead', and for the more active set, Cavendish, an early tobacco type elevated to a trade name. The label depicted a rather sporty rosy-cheeked smoker enjoying 'the smoke of the connoisseur'.

Completing National's stable were their two gold standards. The first of these honoured a racehorse, described as the best mare ever to have graced the track in New Zealand. Desert Gold achieved 36 victories from 59 starts, and her record of 19 successive wins still stands, although now shared with another legend, Gloaming. The champion's name was taken up by the tobacco manufacturer soon after it

On the ball

retired in 1918, but the product survived until the '50s. There is nothing quite so popular as a horse on a winning streak, and so in 1945 Desert Gold tobacco was pushed as 'everybody's favourite'.

By the 1930s Gerhard Husheer had moved his tobacco operations to Nelson. The subsequent economic boost to the area is acknowledged by a Motueka clock tower built in tribute to Husheer. In addition to fruit and hops, the picking of tobacco in Nelson has provided seasonal employment for many.

The emptied tobacco tins have been put to a variety of uses. In some households the 3 lb containers were bound together, covered and cushioned to produce a cheap but comfortable fireside seat.

Until the 1950s the tobacco companies stressed the reputedly 'healthy' aspects of their products. 'Toasted, less nicotine' and 'No sore throat — No cough' were standard claims. Riverhead Gold's 1931 label stated, preposterously, 'Doctors recommend it'. But whatever the habit did for the health of the nation, there is no doubt what it did for its creator, Gerhard Husheer. By 1938 he was one of the wealthiest men in the country, a member of the new upwardly mobile commercial class. His National Tobacco Company buildings were the pride of Napier, and the conditions under which the women operaters worked were described as 'most enlightening'. Husheer himself lived on Napier's Bluff Hill, in a house with two lookout towers — which slipped away in the 1931 earthquake.

Another of Gerhard Husheer's legacies to the nation was the Riverhead Gold girl. The identity of the smiling picker, first seen on the 1924 two-ounce circular tin, and still in use on the Pocket Edition packet, is a subject of debate. But according to Jim Henderson there is no doubt that it is Ruby Simmonds, a Riverhead tobacco picker of Spanish-Portuguese descent. Although the inspiration for one of New Zealand's most popular and enduring trademarks, Ruby was always modest about the details. Perhaps this explains other claims to the title.

More nationalistic than the National Tobacco Company itself was the Dominion, whose most famous trademark at least promoted a local leaf — the Silver Fern. In their new Petone factory

A generation or two ago, every New Zealand adult male seemed to smoke and wear a hat, simultaneously. The cigarette was often a permanent fixture of the bottom lip, even after it had gone out. Smoking also had its own elite subculture: 'rolling your own' was, so the story went, done for the exercise as much as anything else, and there were those who could roll a 'fag' with only one hand. Today, of course, the market is dominated by 'tailor-mades'.

From Riverhead Gold to Coromandel Green.

some 400 hands processed 1,200,000 lb of flue-cured New Zealand tobacco in 1933.

Silver Fern was definitely a bloke's smoke and 1940s advertisements showed servicemen, 'worthy sons of New Zealand', relaxing with a 'roll'. Apart from the distinctive tin and packet (yellow for cut plug and blue for mild smoking tobacco), the do-it-yourselfer could obtain 'many happy rollings' from a half-pound glass jar which provided 'household use when empty'.

The Dominion Company also catered for sportsmen with its Rugby pipe tobacco in the '30s. Spectators at major rugby matches in the past might recall the phenomenon of a myriad exhaled puffs from a crowd of smokers.

As well as National and Dominion

there was the Imperial Tobacco Company. Its blue Melrose, dating from the early '30s, had obvious class — recalling an ancient Scottish town once associated with Sir Walter Scott. By contrast, the Bears brand had an identity problem — its label was graced by an elephant.

Finally there was an Auckland company which brought us a more international flavour. Combining mainly Kentucky and Virginia leaves with the pick of the local crop, the St James's Tobacco Co. exposed New Zealand smokers to modern trends. Their du Maurier was the first filter-tip cigarette made in this country. The now-forgotten First Lord was the first king-size, and Albany combined the two in the first local king-size filter. But indigenous tastes were not overlooked by St James's

with its Kauri Virginia tobacco. The red tin said 'Kauri Stands for Quality' although by then most of our kauri stands were gone.

Some modern horticulturalists have taken a leaf, as it were, from Brett's authoritative *Colonial Guide* and offered New Zealand a totally different sort of smoke. The settlers' manual recommended a flax-like plant used in the textile industry as a local crop. It adapted readily and had seeds 'sweet to taste' which were excellent for caged birds and poultry. Hemp, or *Cannabis sativa*, was to become a lucrative, and illegal, cash crop in the 1960s. Riverhead once had its 'Gold', but Coromandel now had its 'Green'.

On the ball

'Now is the Hour. . .'

*I*f New Zealand can claim a music of its own, then it is probably the mixture of the country's two main, diverse traditions.

The first music heard in New Zealand was made by the Maori. They had few instruments and their inspiration was the sounds of nature. The results probably bore little similarity to 'authentic' Maori music of today, but we will never know for sure. Captain Cook noted the precision of Maori singing in 1770. Three years later he demonstrated to a Maori audience a sample of European music, in the form of bagpipes, fife and drum. The latter attracted most attention for the pre-European Maori had no such instrument. Neither did they possess strings, but for melodic purposes they had flutes. Trumpets were

made from converted conch shells, or wood, as were bullroarers and children's novelty instruments. But perhaps the most distinctive feature of traditional Maori music is the use of the unaccompanied voice, a practice largely outmoded by the arrival of the guitar. The common form was the waiata, or song of love or lament, still retained for ceremonial occasions.

Waiata became the name of the 1981 album by New Zealand's most successful musical group to date, Split Enz, who thoughtfully re-entitled it *Corroborree* for the Australian market. But an earlier waiata was to become one of the best-known songs of all time. In about 1913 Maewa Kaihau and Clement Scott wrote the Maori lyrics for *Po Ata Rau*, which was translated into English and

published in 1936. Gracie Fields then popularised it among the troops during the Second World War, and eventually Bing Crosby got to hear of it. His version of *Now is the Hour* became a million-seller in 1948.

The early European explorers may have introduced a little light music to New Zealand but it was the military who best promoted it. The first such concert was given in the Bay of Islands in 1845 by the band of the 58th Regiment, otherwise known as 'the Black Cuffs'. Then, in 1859, the Taranaki Volunteer Rifles formed the country's first volunteer brass band. To cater for the growing popularity of this type of music, national brass band championships were instituted, beginning at Christchurch in 1880. Another form

The bodgie — and his female counterpart the widgie — was a social phenomenon of the late fifties through early sixties. Springing from a growing youth 'revolt' that was driven by increasing financial independence, personal mobility, and, *of course,* rock and roll and teenage movie stars.

This new-found freedom, however, caused a great deal of public (i.e. older generational) concern. Indeed the problem led to a number of studies and books, the most well known of which locally was *The Bodgie — A study in abnormal psychology.* Written by A. E. Manning, an Auckland psychologist, following his research in both New Zealand and Australia, the book was published in 1958.

Among other observations, Manning noted the characteristic dress of the bodgie:

'In their habits all followed a social pattern. The males wore unusual and exaggerated haircuts, following the styles made popular by various film stars. All went to extremes in the style of suits worn. The trousers were all much tighter in the legs than is usual. Some favoured extreme shortness of leg, exposing garishly coloured socks. Coats, when worn, were fuller in cut and much longer than is normal by conservative standards, while all favoured brightly coloured shirts, pull-overs or wind-breakers, and neckerchiefs. The ''Bodgies'' have reverted to the colour of the Elizabethan age.

'The girls were rather more standardised in their dress. Hair was worn drawn tightly back and tied in a tail or was worn in a bushy wind-swept style fringing carelessly over the forehead, showing neither the artistry nor the diversity of style manifested by the youths. On the average the girls were more

THE PROBLEM

uniformly drab than the boys with their exotic colours. All were characterised by rather louder voices when together, but were all quiet in manner during interviews.'

A new slant on an old theme, 'bodgies' were simply the latest in the line from 'yahoos' and 'larrikins'. And, in hindsight, bodgie transgressions were pretty mild by the standards of today's hoons. The word bodgie itself seems to derive from American slang for a young male jitterbug.

that has always been popular in New Zealand is Scottish pipe band music. The country's first such band was the Caledonian, of Southland, formed in 1896, and today there are more of these bands per head of population here than there are in Scotland.

Early European settlers had to bring their own instruments. Gilbert Mair did so in 1827, and his 1740 Broadwood Square Grand piano — the country's oldest — is now in the Treaty House at Waitangi. But from 1861 musical New Zealanders were able to purchase their requirements from Charles Beggs's new store in Dunedin. The business is still going, with the addition of Wiseman's, and has branches throughout the country.

The new settler in the antipodes was not altogether starved of European culture. Beginning about the turn of the century New Zealand received regular visits from such musical luminaries as Dame Nellie Melba (1903), Ignace Paderewski (1904), Dame Clara Butt (1908), the American bandleader John Philip Sousa (1911), the Irish tenor John McCormack (1913), the 150-strong Italian Grand Opera Company (1917), Anna Pavlova (1926) and 17 year-old Yehudi Menuhin in 1935.

In spite of such distinguished visitors, the most popular form of musical entertainment during the early 20th century was the musical comedy. These lighthearted and colourful presentations were as much a feature of colonial life as they were in England. The theme songs from *The Geisha, The Merry Widow* and *Madame Butterfly,* for example, were heard in the streets and their costumes influenced local fashion. This genre of entertainment made a household name of Gladys Moncrieff, who trod the boards between 1924 and 1961. During the course of her marathon career another variation on the musical comedy emerged. This had American rather than English origins, and made fortunes for such composers as George Gershwin, Jerome Kern and Rogers and Hammerstein. *Rose Marie, No No Nanette* and *The Student Prince* were perennial favourites, but the giant of them all was *The Desert Song,* capitalising on the vogue for things Middle Eastern.

During the Second World War there was a sudden injection of contemporary American culture into New Zealand. The GIs brought their own music, introducing

On the ball

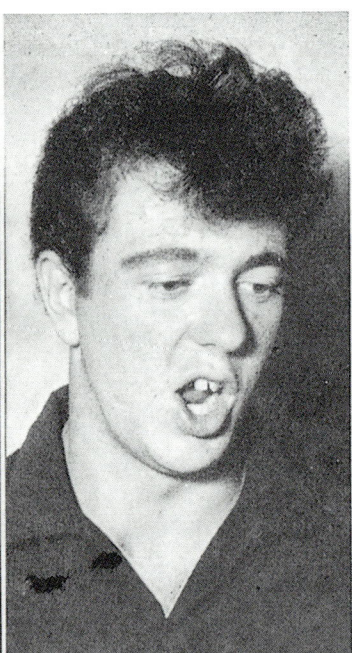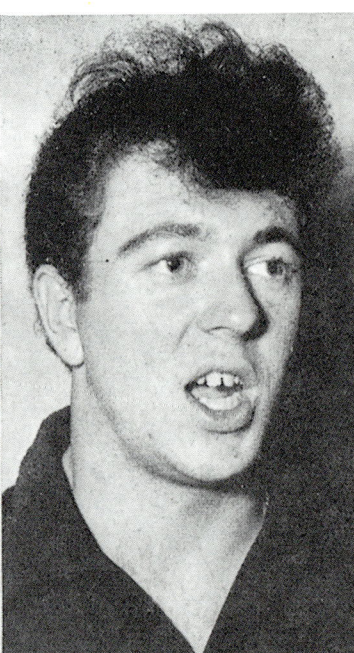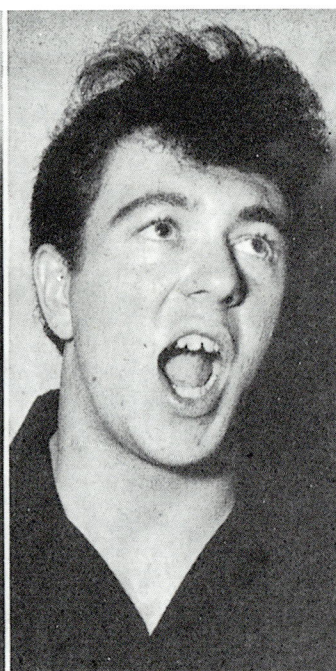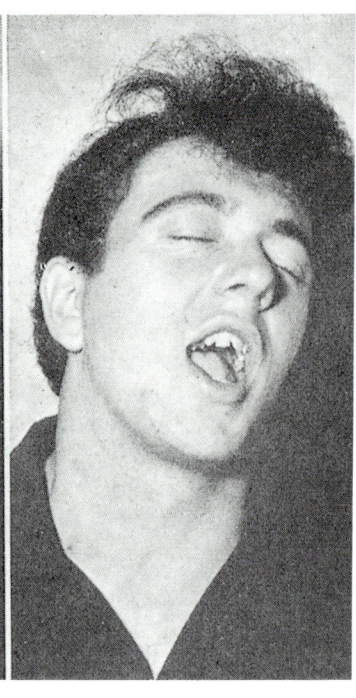

Johnny Devlin.

the South Pacific to swing bands and the art of jitter-bugging. But by the end of the 1940s the momentum was lost: the urgency of the 'swing' had become diluted to a sentimental mush. Perhaps the musical pits were reached in 1953 when 'I Saw Mommy Kissing Santa Claus' and 'How Much Is That Doggy in the Window' both hit the top, as it were.

All the while there was a new form of music and there was another force to be reckoned with — the first generation of so-called 'teenagers', the legacy of the postwar baby boom. Their demand was for a sound to call their own, to set them apart from the blandness of their elders. This found a perfect expression in a combination of traditional negro blues and country and western music. With the addition of a no-nonsense beat, rock

'n' roll was born.

The honour of providing the first such teenage anthem went to an unlikely star, an overweight singer called Bill Haley. He and his Comets recorded the landmark 'Rock Around the Clock' which rocketed to the top of the charts in 1955 and kept coming back for more. It monopolised the American charts for eight weeks, to be eventually displaced by the somewhat regressive 'Yellow Rose of Texas'. But by now the message had reached New Zealand and the attention of the HMV company. East Coast-born country and western singer Johnny Cooper — known as the 'Maori Cowboy' — was despatched to the studio with his Range Riders for a quick cover version. In at the deep end, their first attempt at rock 'n' roll sank without trace, but not

before creating a record of another sort. It was quite possibly the first rock 'n' roll recording made outside the United States — decisively beating the likes of Britain's Cliff Richard and Tommy Steele and Australia's Johnny O'Keefe.

In 1956 the film of the song 'Rock Around the Clock' introduced New Zealand to the Haley original, and the nation's youth were quickly converted. They now had a whole new style, from music to stove-pipe trousers and luminous socks. But the authorities were not so sure: all they could see were social problems associated with the bodgies and widgies now hanging around the milkbars.

New Zealand's first rock 'n' rollers were enthusiastic, if not entirely original. Other countries quickly groomed their

own Elvis Presley equivalents, and we had a creditable substitute in Johnny Devlin. This son of Raetihi (later of Gonville, Wanganui) made his musical debut at the age of 13 at the Wanganui Opera House. Beginning at talent quests throughout the central North Island, Devlin developed a repertoire (and hairstyle) with Elvis as his obvious role model. He began his recording career with a reworking of the King's 'Lawdy Miss Clawdy'. Along with a later improved version the disc sold over 100,000 copies — the biggest ever sales for a single record released in New Zealand. 'Lawdy Miss Clawdy' was followed in quick succession by other covers: 'Stagger Lee', 'Slippin' Around' and 'Straight Skirt'.

By early 1958 Devlin had arrived at Auckland's Jive Centre and New Zealand soon had its very own 'king'. There followed a year of hysteria — from fan clubs to torn shirts. Devlin packed theatres throughout the country. More than 10,000 enthusiastic fans were drawn to Auckland's Western Springs, but by mid 1959 it was all over. Johnny Devlin and his backing group, the Devils, crossed the Tasman. The phenomenon had passed, but it had left its mark on New Zealand in more ways than one.

Elvis never made it to New Zealand — one of the few superstars of the business who didn't. However, plenty of lesser beings flocked to these shores, Bobby Rydell included. His arrival at New Plymouth airport created a local uproar when an over-enthusiastic fan managed to place her stiletto heel on the foot of a local newspaper reporter. The incident was a catalyst for considerable pent-up feeling about teenage decadence and the demise of civilisation as we know it. For his part, Bobby Rydell was really Robert Ridarelli, and his songs were hardly offensive.

Although lacking Elvis's hallmark pelvic thrusts, Rydell scored well in this country with such teen ballads as 'Wild One' and 'Volare'. Later this immaculately groomed all-American boy had his stage name immortalised as Rydell High School in *Grease*, the play (and film) that nostalgically reflected on the halcyon days of rock 'n' roll. But these times were more than a little confusing.

As well as Rydell, New Zealand's record bins were once regularly filled

On the ball

This visit to New Zealand by the Beatles, now at the peak of their international career, illustrates the importance of this country in the world wide "show business" scene. In presenting the Beatles, Kerridge Odeon offers this pictorial record — the first section being devoted to those artists appearing on the show — the second section being a close look at the events leading up to, and the ultimate triumphs of this fabulous group. And now let's relax and enjoy the swinging sounds of these four British bombs called the Beatles, as they bring us the hits that have made them famous, illustrating a talent that has the world laughing, swinging and singing!

with other Bobbys — Darin, Vinton and Vee. The first (born Walden Cassotto) struck in the '50s with 'Splish Splash', 'Dream Lover' and 'Mack the Knife', and returned with a vengeance in 1966 with 'If I Were a Carpenter'. Bobby Vee was really Robert Velline, and he charted here with 'Rubber Ball', 'Devil or Angel' and 'The Night Has a Thousand Eyes'. Finally, Bobby Vinton was distinguished by sentimentality, as oozed by 'Roses Are Red', and an extensive repertoire of songs whose titles all included the world 'blue'.

Having suffered Bobby Rydell, the concerned citizens of New Plymouth had another shock when the Pretty Things came to town in the mid '60s. This rag-tag outfit shared the bill with Sandie Shaw, who warbled shoeless and blinded by the footlights. However, the not-so-

Pretty Things — their name inspired by a Bo Diddley song — played an altogether dirtier type of music. Their drummer, Viv Prince, appeared to be sick on stage, as well as almost setting fire to the Opera House curtains. Now categorised as proto-punk, the antics of the Pretty Things were soon forgotten when punk proper and heavy metal hit the country.

Rock 'n' roll was an American invention that fuelled an English musical invasion of New Zealand in the 1960s. By repackaging rhythm and blues for popular consumption, the Beatles struck like no other musical phenomenon — before or since. In the process they created career opportunities for many of their less talented colleagues. New Zealand thus received a wide range of

rock 'n' roll imports, some later ascending to rock 'n' roll immortality, while others were never heard of again. Contenders for the latter category were the Honeycombs, best remembered for their female drummer, 'Honey' Lantree. However, they did manage one huge hit here in 1964, the strident 'Have I the Right?'

Stayers by comparison were the Who, preceded to New Zealand by a certain destructive reputation. With this in mind the Wellington Town Hall provided the group with only second-best microphones. The Who destroyed them anyway. At the lower end of rock's destruction scale was P. J. Proby — Jim Smith to his friends — whose trousers could always be relied upon to rip, particularly during a deep and

Ray Columbus.

Dinah Lee.

Mr Lee Grant.

Sandy Edmonds.

meaningful version of 'Maria' rendered from the crouching position.

When the Rolling Stones made a triumphant return to Auckland in 1973, Mick Jagger's sheets were auctioned for charity — courtesy of the Hotel Intercontinental. The Stones had already toured New Zealand in 1965, in the unlikely company of Roy Orbison. The 'Big O' was the master of the melancholy ballad, climaxing with 'Pretty Woman'. His style was not unlike a fellow American, Gene Pitney, a regular visitor here in the '60s who was hardly ever out of our top 20. Gene tearjerked his way through such pitiful platters as '24 Hours from Tulsa', 'Princess in Rags' and 'Backstage'.

Just as Johnny Cooper had borrowed from Bill Haley, and Johnny Devlin from

Elvis, the 1960s was a period of cover versions of overseas songs by aspiring New Zealand artists. Obscure imports provided the likes of Ray Columbus with his 1965 Loxene Gold Disc Winner, 'Till We Kissed'. To be fair, this song was originally entitled 'Where Have You Been?'. It became Ray Columbus and the Invaders' finest hour, selling some 50,000 copies, but the band split up soon afterwards.

Their recording career had begun, rather disastrously, in 1963 with their own composition. Thereafter they stuck to covers, from obscure Danish instrumentals ('Kupow') to proven lyrics by Lennon and McCartney ('I Wanna Be Your Man'). The band further capitalised on Beatlemania by switching from being Elvis-imitators to mods, and recording an

anthem in celebration.

An English composition, 'She's a Mod', catapulted them to the top of all Australasia. With the band's demise in 1965, two members crossed the Tasman to join another great New Zealand rock institution — Max Merritt and the Meteors. This band was born in Christchurch in the late '50s and owed both its name and style to Bill Haley's Comets. Nevertheless their first records were original compositions and significant local hits, including a possibly Haley-inspired 'Kiss Curl' and a pre-Beatles 'Get a Haircut'.

In late 1963 the band went to Australia and acquired a loyal following based on cover versions of rock classics. Some 20 years later the original Meteors have long gone, but the irrepressible Max

On the ball

'The sound of modern radio, home of the Good Guys.' It is to the original 'good guys' of Radio Hauraki that credit is due for the introduction of private radio in New Zealand. But it took them nearly four years of battling bureaucracy, of law suits, debt and disaster to do it. Twenty-five years ago radio in this country was monopolised by the then New Zealand Broadcasting Corporation, a state-controlled organisation. While it was theoretically possible to gain a private broadcasting warrant, powerful political interests made this unachievable in practice.

When Radio Hauraki was formed, for the purpose of broadcasting pop music to the youth audience — a sector of the listening public ignored by the government stations — the problem of access to a warrant led to Hauraki's directors putting together a floating radio station, aboard the good ship *Tiri*, to broadcast to Auckland listeners from beyond the then three-mile limit of law.

The adventure for Radio Hauraki's 'pirates' began in late 1966 when they finally put to sea after last-minute official harassment and arrest. It didn't stop there. For the next four years the fight for independent private radio was a saga of law suits, bureaucratic stalling, debt, toppled radio masts and shipwreck. It was also a story of huge, enthusiastic support from tens of thousands of listeners, of increasing advertising income,

The MV 'Tiri'.

and of a revolution in radio in this country. When the Hauraki pirates came ashore in mid 1970 after 1111 days at sea and having been finally granted a private licence, they had helped to usher in a new era in entertainment and communications.

Radio Hauraki

Merritt still performs in Australia.

New Zealand can view with a certain smugness the success of its musicians on the other side of the Tasman. However, there is one genre of music at which Australia excels. In the area of popular humour, based more on hyperbole than fact, certain Australian originals have enjoyed international success. Compared to the likes of 'Tie Me Kangaroo Down, Sport' and 'The Pub With No Beer', New Zealand's own comedy output is rather modest, although Kiwi recording artists have had fun with such national institutions as the Auckland to Wellington 'Limited' ('Taumarunui on the Main Trunk Line'), rural necessities ('The Dog Dosing Strip at Dunsandel'), social events ('Down the Hall on a Saturday Night') and our most famous marine animal ('Opo the Crazy Dolphin').

Of less consequence were the strictly regional efforts, often inspired by major sporting events. In the late 1950s Taranaki rugby supporters were urged on to successful defences of the Ranfurly Shield with their mascot's song, 'Ferdinand, Ferdinand' ('with your fifteen men ...'), sung to the tune of 'Robin Hood, Robin Hood' ('with your band of men...').

Very occasionally national pride might break out and be expressed on record, such as the little-known 'Hillary Song'. By Jimmy Fitzpatrick, accompanied by Allan Siddall 'and his Strict Tempo Music', this ditty managed to combine such lofty themes as Queen and Country with a suitable rhyme for 'Everest':

Hil-la-ry we're so proud of you
So proud of you, so proud of you
You climbed up, up where clouds
touch the blue
And so we take our hats off to you
Through forty degrees below zero
You proved that you're our true blue
hero
You knew you would never rest
Until you conquered Mount Ev-er-est
Now you've done it
Reached the summit
Won it for the red, white and blue
The coronation population
Cheers for you congratulations
Hil-la-ry, we're proud of you.

The Howard Morrison Quartet.

Choice of the professionals!
TEX MORTON GUITARS

Superb tone and attractive appearance make Tex Morton Guitars the natural choice of professionals.

Tex Morton can develop your latent musical talents quickly. Inability to read music is no drawback. Why delay any longer — learn now about Tex Morton's postal lessons for the Guitar.

Fred Dagg.

Back in the mainstream, musical humour in New Zealand was once synonymous with the Howard Morrison Quartet. This group was formed in the late '50s and became a national family favourite as a result of home-made parodies of other peoples' songs. Thus, Johnny Horton's 1959 'Battle of New Orleans' became, down here, 'The Battle of the Waikato', and Lonnie Donegan's 'My Old Man's a Dustman' of the following year was elevated to 'My Old Man's an All Black'. The latter made reference to the all-white All Black rugby tour to South Africa that year. The line 'There's no Horis in this scrum' reflected the level of the average New Zealander's concern. The quartet's version of Ray Steven's 'Ahab the Arab' would be equally out of place by today's

standards: 'Mori the Hori' it was called. Nevertheless, during the early 60s such humour seemed perfectly acceptable — and appreciated by Maori and Pakeha alike — drawing 20,000 fans to Western Springs stadium. Another notable cheap-shot novelty song was a parody by Lou and Simon. *West Side Story*'s 'I Wanna Be in America' was converted, with 'America' replaced by 'a Maori car'.

Within a decade New Zealand had more serious concerns. Agriculture was undergoing a major shake-up as Britain eased into the EEC. Farmers became vulnerable and were no longer a privileged class. They now became the butt of black-singleted comic, John Clark, better known as Fred Dagg. In catchy little ditties he made droll fun of the rural sector, or offered hope when all

else seemed lost, as in 'You Don't Know How Lucky You Are'.

Musically speaking, New Zealand has pounced on every fad going and used it for its own purposes. Long before even rock 'n' roll was thought of, country and western music was well established down here. C&W's spiritual home, Nashville, Tennessee, had been inspiring Kiwi cowboys as early as the '30s. Nelson-born Tex Morton (actually Bob Lane) was our first and greatest exponent of the style, eventually crossing the Tasman to become a country legend. Later came Cole Wilson and his Tumbleweeds, a quartet whose middle-of-the-range music was regular evening fare on provincial radio stations in the '50s. Also maintaining the cowboy image were such good ol' boys as Garner Wayne and his

On the ball

The most distinctive feature of New Zealand music is its Pacific connection, forged from the musicality of the indigenous Maori, and now increasingly mixed with other Pacific influences. Kiri Te Kanawa and the late Inia Te Wiata sang their way to international recognition in opera, while in a more popular vein, Maori entertainers like John Rowles have reinterpreted aspects of their musical heritage. Indeed the story of original popular music in New Zealand is largely one of Maori versatility, from the Howard Morrison Quartet to the more recent chart-topping *Poi E* performed by Dalvanius Prime and the Patea Maori Club, reggae by Herbs and Polynesian rhythm from Ardijah.

Herbs.

Saddle Pals and Rusty Greaves. More recently our country hall of fame has been extended to include such household names as John Hore, Patsy Riggir and Suzanne Prentice.

Overseas rock 'n' roll groups set the standard in New Zealand. Cliff Richard's original backing group, the Shadows, were once the model for our own Meteors and Invaders. Later the Beatles put the seal of approval on the line-up of three guitarists and a drummer — not to mention mop-top haircuts and natty suits. In stark sartorial contrast were the Rolling Stones, Animals and Pretty Things who provided the mould for innumerable hopeful R&B outfits. This form of homage has now been taken to its logical conclusion with the recent appearance in Australia of an unashamed cover group, the Rolling Clones.

The flow of rock 'n' roll influence has not been altogether one way. Recently, New Zealander and ex-Split Enz Neil Finn has achieved considerable chart success in the USA with his group Crowded House. And some 20 years earlier, John Rowles of Kawerau almost got to the top in Britain. In 1966 he went to Australia and changed his name to the alien-sounding Ja-Ar. Two years later, as John Rowles again, his 'If I Only Had Time' rose to number three in Britain. 'Not a Word to Mary' followed it to number 12, and established him as a singer in the mould of Tom Jones and Engelbert Humperdinck. A later song, 'Cheryl Moana Marie', was named for his sister. Back home this was parodied as 'Share Your Marijuana with Me'.

Middle-of-the-road music, as associated with the likes of John Rowles, finds a ready market in New Zealand. It was a 1967 song by Engelbert Humperdinck that became something of an alternative national anthem. The flip-side of his first, huge single 'Release Me' was 'Ten Guitars', a sing-along favourite at New Zealand social occasions ever since.

At the heart of rock 'n' roll lies the dance, the obvious inspiration for many of its songs. Some of the more basic lyrics have sufficient ambiguity to imply a more horizontal activity, also popular with teenagers. In 1957, in 'Wake Up Little Susie', Don and Phil Everly sang of a post-coital nap that would get both in 'trouble deep'. Ten years later there was absolutely no doubt what 'Let's Spend

the Night Together' meant, so the NZBC banished the Rolling Stones' single from the airwaves. Neither did they appreciate Manfred Mann's number two hit in Britain, 'If You Gotta Go, Go Now' whose next line went 'or else you gotta stay all night'.

But in the late '60s it was political comment as much as sex that upset the Broadcasting Corporation. While the Vietnam War dragged on Manfred Mann's 'With God on Our Side' (a Bob Dylan original) and Donovan's 'Universal Soldier' were not to be heard on local radio. Fortunately for the enthusiast, there were Australian stations which came in clearly and were happy to play just about anything. However, New Zealand performers still had to mind their language in 1977. Urban layabout

Neville Purvis ('at your service'), a.k.a. Arthur Baysting, with the record 'Give Me Money' to his credit, also managed his own television series, briefly. In the closing moments of the final show he uttered the unforgiveable expletive — thereby both creating local history and destroying a career.

Despite its size New Zealand has managed to produce regional preferences in popular music. The home of country and western here is somewhere in Southland, and the surfing resorts of the North Island were once the haunts of Beach Boys fans. But over the years radio request sessions have revealed some more unusual preferences. Such 'songs' as the yodelling 'Auctioneer' and 'Love in a Fowlhouse' may have owed their appeal to a mixture of novelty and

nostalgia. But the spoken 'Deck of Cards' was definitely another story. Perhaps such a practical solution to a spiritual problem was something that New Zealanders could appreciate.

Of all the exponents of popular music in this country, the most original have been Split Enz. They began life somewhere between O'Rorke Hall and the Wynyard Tavern — in Symonds Street, Auckland — and the Elam School of Fine Arts, across the road. Two years later they abbreviated their Ends to Enz, but personnel changes would be more a feature of the band's history. Although much loved at home — and Australia — they were perhaps too advanced for international acceptance. 'I Got You', from their 1979 *True Colours* album, was more infectious than zany and should

On the ball

Split Enz — the mid 1970s lineup (left to right from the back): Philip Judd, Eddie Rayner, Wally Wilkinson, Emylyn Crowther, Tim Finn, Michael Chunn, Noel Crombie.

From left: Tim Finn, Eddie Rayner, Nigel Griggs, Noel Crombie, Neil Finn.

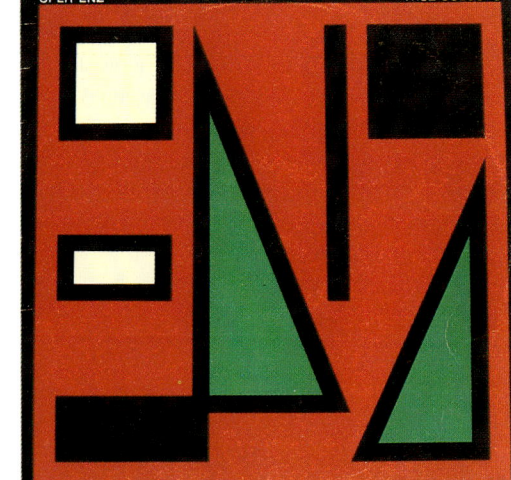

have topped charts everywhere. Equally unfortunate was the timing of their 1982 single, 'Six Months in a Leaky Boat': the BBC refused to play it on account of the Falklands War. Nevertheless, the song remains one of the nation's finest achievements, with such classic antipodean references as 'the tyranny of distance'.

Few true fans will forget the 1984 'Enz with a Bang' tour and the patriotism evoked by the line 'Ao-tea-roa, rugged individual'. Pursuing the nautical theme, and also from their penultimate *Time and Tide* album, was Tim Finn's autobiographical 'Haul Away'. This is a worthy addition to our catalogue of songs of small-town New Zealand, telling of his origins in Te Awamutu.

Rock 'n' roll was once the exclusive preserve of the young, but it has since been institutionalised. Its effectiveness as a communicator could not pass unnoticed by the advertising industry. Thus, some of rock's classic moments now promote Telecom's phones and exhort us to 'Love Hertz'. Even 1964 vintage Rolling Stones is not immune, except that what's 'All Over Now' is a deodorant, not a relationship. We can only hope that, in the spirit of Split Enz, our musicians keep at least one step ahead of boring respectability.

Circumstances surrounding the origin of New Zealand's national dessert have long been the subject of contention, but without argument is its inspiration — the Russian ballerina Anna Pavlova, who toured Australia and New Zealand in 1925-26.

While the *Australian Encyclopaedia* credits the meringue concoction to a Perth chef, the dancer's biographer, Keith Money, is adamant that it was a Wellington hotel chef who, during the New Zealand leg of the tour, first made the dish. The story goes that the chef saw Pavlova dressed in a tutu draped in cabbage roses made from green silk and was inspired to invent a dish that re-created the effect. Hence the meringue case, as an attempt at the shape of the tutu, and the whipped cream, the froth of the tutu's net. The use of pieces of chinese gooseberry (now kiwifruit) was of course to echo the roses.

Keith Money describes the original recipe — with the only permissible fruit flavours being passionfruit in the cream and the kiwifruit on top — as 'a brilliant simulation of Pavlova's personality. The Australian habit of using Golden Queen peaches, and the Long Island one of using strawberries ... makes the thing far too sickly sweet, the antithesis of Pavlova's performing style which was invariably praised for its subtlety and strangeness. The whole point about Pavlova was that she could take something potentially sweet and sentimental, like the ''Gavotte'', or ''Dance of the Hours'', and inject it with wit, or other-worldliness or whatever ... and thus drag it right out of the commonplace. And the original chef matched her exactly.'

'The Incomparable Pavlova': an informal snapshot of the dancer in the garden of her London home, 1930.

ANNA PAVLOVA
GRAND OPERA HOUSE

The Saturday night social or dance was a feature of the country scene in particular and an event that became the subject of one of Peter Cape's most famous songs, 'Down the Hall on a Saturday Night'. In the following excerpt, Wellington broadcaster Linsay Yeo describes what such dances were like in his own home town of Waianiwa. In this instance he is remembering the annual Plunket Ball:

'Now they were real dances. The organising committee was thorough. No-one ever forgot to turn the hall heaters on at three o'clock in the afternoon and the highly polished dance floor always had a perfectly distributed sprinkling of powder, and the *Lest We Forget* commemoration roll of honour plaque was always illuminated and its plush scarlet drapes parted neatly.

'Everyone arrived at eight o'clock sharp and looked wonderful. The ladies had little waists and rouged cheeks and lots of petticoats and the men had natty pin-striped suits with smart tie–pins and RSA badges and neatly brylcreamed short-back-and-sides.

'Everyone stood patriotically as the wheezy accordion band solemnly delivered 'God Save the Queen' and the jovial Master of Ceremonics, who'd been a popular fixture at these balls for 20 years, welcomed the villagers with the order of dances for the next four hours. From the opening circular waltz to the Gypsy Tap, Maxina, the popular Gay Gordons, Valetta, Foxtrot, Quickstep and the evening's highlight, the boisterous Highland Schottische.

'Everyone knew about, but didn't mind, the men slipping outside, to their cars for the occasional beer or nip of scotch. And the suppers were sumptuous. Long trestled tables groaned with cheerios, dagwood sandwiches, chocolate eclairs, cream cakes and every other home-baked delicacy imaginable. But not before you'd danced the supper waltz with the partner who'd come to the ball with you. On the dot of midnight the revellers crossed arms and joined hands for 'Auld Lang Syne' followed by another chorus of 'God Save the Queen'. Things like that were done properly in Waianiwa.'

Beach and *Bach*

Beach and bach

The northbound Daylight Express 1930.

Through to the end of the 1950s most long-distance travel by Kiwis was either by train or ship. Air travel in the fifties was not yet competitive with ocean liners such as the *Wanganella*, *Dominion Monarch* and the 'Rangi' ships on their regular runs between New Zealand and Australia and the UK. Certainly, domestic air travel was eclipsed by New Zealand Railways and Road Services and the interisland ferries.

Railway's steel roads could take you just about anywhere. Thanks to the ambitious public works projects of the late 1870s, the country's main and provincial centres were linked by a network of rail. In the process a lot of dense bush had been cleared and some extremely complex engineering achieved. Massive viaducts were built spanning

numerous ravines, but most remarkable was the Raurimu Spiral which completed the last section of the Main Trunk in the central North Island. To overcome some otherwise impassable terrain, a complete spiral involving three horseshoe curves and two tunnels was created.

Far steeper than the famous spiral was the iron road connecting the Hutt Valley and the Wairarapa — the Rimutaka Incline. Over the notoriously windy range of the same name, the Incline required a gradient of 1 in 14. It was in operation between 1878 and 1955, when it was replaced by an 8.8 kilometre-long tunnel.

For the true enthusiast the romance of rail began to die in 1936. It was then that the petrol-powered railcar began to replace the familiar workhorse the K-

class steam locomotive. A few years later the Wellington surburban lines were electrified, and in the early '50s this was extended to the Hutt Valley. By 1955 railcars were phasing out provincial express services altogether, their red streamlined shapes and Cyclops lights above the cabs spreading into every region in the country. Diesel locos followed and in 1971 the last working steamer — a Ja-class hauling between Christchurch and Dunedin — brought an end to an era when it completed its last trip that year.

The automobile came to New Zealand in the early 1900s and the country quickly came to grips with it. With the new mobility the car afforded, New Zealanders could really get around. Shopping excursions and commuting to

LAKE WANAKA

Scenic Trip
by Train &
Railway Motor

NEW ZEALAND RAILWAYS
SAFETY · COMFORT · ECONOMY

NEW ZEALAND

Come out for
LABOUR DAY

BY
TRAIN

Beach and bach

Steam locomotive power lingered on in New Zealand until 1971, a couple of decades after the introduction of diesel locos with their promises of lower manning levels and easier running. The rapid demise of steam was slowed somewhat, however, by the changing over of many of the old coal-fired boilers to oil burning. Eventually, though, and despite the greater ability of steam power to provide the ready and rapid acceleration that is ideal in a geography offering numerous curves and steep grades, the switch to DA and DX locos was complete. Magnificent J and K-class engines, among others, drew their last breaths as the fires in their innards went out, and expired quietly on neglected sidings.

J-class loco.

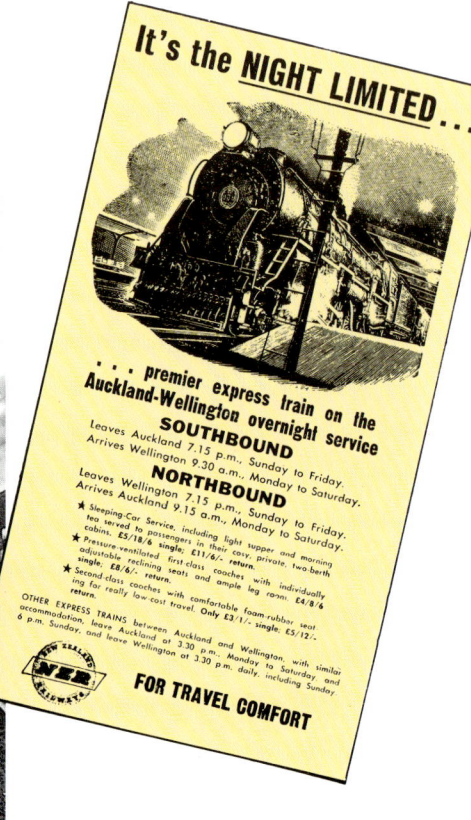

work aside, Sunday drives, picnics and beach visits were now possible. But perhaps the big event was the annual holiday, a stay with relatives or, alternatively, avoiding them by going to the beach or bach. Certain favoured holiday spots became regular haunts, such as Nelson, Oakura, Taupo, Whangamata and 'the Mount' (Maunganui). On the way there New Zealanders became more familiar with sizeable chunks of their country and, years later, certain roads are guaranteed to recall uncomfortable journeys — especially if a gorge was involved.

No reasonable trip could avoid at least one of these — snaking beside a river with precipitous cliffs at either side. Taranaki had the Awakino Gorge, with Mount Messenger and the Mahoenui Hills

on either side for good measure, and Manawatu had its own gorge providing access to Hawke's Bay. Elsewhere there were the Buller and Waioeka gorges, and Arthur's Pass and the Mamukus. A particularly major undertaking used to be the Napier-Taupo road, which once kept two intrepid motorists busy for three days in 1903. In the 1960s this route was finally sealed and straightened out. Another route still remains less removed from its own originally awesome reputation: the arduous route from Taihape to Hastings, euphemistically known as 'Gentle Annie'.

The 1920s were barnstorming days of aviation as daring young men and women set all sorts of local records. The first official airmail was delivered from Auckland to Dargaville in 1919, and the

following year Cook Strait was conquered in an Avro 540K. 1921 saw Foveaux Strait fall, as well as recording the first flight between Wellington and Auckland. But the real hero of the air was an Australian, Charles Kingsford-Smith, who was first across the Tasman. His three-engined monoplane *Southern Cross* took nearly 14½ hours from Sydney to Christchurch's Wigram airport.

Shortly after this pioneering period an infant commercial aviation industry gave ordinary citizens the chance to fly. A number of small airlines had been formed around the country and in 1945 three of these, Union Airways, Cook Strait Airways and Air Travel NZ Ltd were nationalised to become NAC. Operations began with the ever-practical DC-3 Dakota and progressed to the

Rail travel has contributed a fair amount of material to our national folk history, and perhaps best known is the refreshment-stop scramble that was part of travelling on the Main Trunk lines of both islands. With the abolition of the dining-car in 1917, rail travellers found themselves deposited instead at rail station refreshment rooms and these brief stops — of around 10 minutes or so — became part of the inconvenience, discomfort and, at times, adventure that was rail travel. On the North Island's 'Night Limited' these stops — at Taihape, Frankton, Taumarunui and Palmerston North — were places where, in the middle of nowhere it seemed, you came to, briefly, for sustenance before falling back on your hired pillow for further fitful sleep.

As the train slowed down to a stop at the platform it was a mad scramble off the train to purchase a pie or sandwich and the obligatory cuppa, the tea and coffee already milked and poured from vast stainless steel teapots. Everything, cups and all, was carried back on board. Some time later a guard would work his way down the carriages with a wire basket, or kero-tin made into a box, retrieving the famous no-nonsense Crown Lynn railway cups.

Legendary among these stops was Taumarunui and in the late fifties the canteen there was immortalised in a song by writer Peter Cape. The song tells of a passenger who, because of his love for one of the women serving the refreshments, becomes a fireman on a steam train in order to spend time with her. Alas, she switches to the day shift.

The refreshment scramble passed away, sadly regretted, on 21 February 1975, the date on which the Taumarunui canteen sold its last pie.

Memorable, too, was the overnight ferry service between Wellington and Lyttelton aboard the likes of the *Hinemoa, Maori* or *Rangatira*. Tucked up in cosy berths, passengers were treated to the romance of a sea voyage as their ship plied the north Canterbury and Marlborough coastlines from one island to the other. Around dawn you would be awoken by a white-jacketed steward bearing a thick porcelain cup of hot tea and a round wine or digestive biscuit. Then it was up on deck to watch as your destination came into sight. In the jet age of the sixties it was a mode of travel whose days were numbered. However, the end of the 63-year-old night service came with a bang, not a whimper, when the *Wahine,* on 10 April 1968, was driven on to Barrett Reef at the entrance of Wellington Harbour during the monumental storm that broke over that Easter weekend.

Taumarunui

I'm an ordinary joker, getting old before me time
For me heart's in Taumarunui on the Main Trunk Line
Taumarunui, Taumarunui
Taumarunui on the Main Trunk Line.

You can get to Taumarunui going north or going south
And you end up there at midnight and you've cinders in your mouth
You've cinders in your whiskers and a cinder in your eye
So you pop off to refreshments for a cup of tea and pie
In Taumarunui on the Main Trunk Line.

There's a sheila in refreshments and she's pouring cups of tea
And my heart jumps like a rabbit when she pours a cup for me
She's h..ir of flamin' yellow and a mouth of flamin' red
And I'll love that flamin' sheila till I'm up and gone and dead
In Taumarunui, Taumarunui
Taumarunui on the Main Trunk Line.

You can get a job in Wellington or get a job up North
But you can't in Taumarunui though you try for all you're worth
If I want to see this sheila then I've got to take a train
Got ten minutes for refreshments, then they cart me off again
From Taumarunui, Taumarunui
Taumarunui on the Main Trunk Line.

Well, they took me on as fireman on the Limited Express
And I thought that she'd be jake but now she's all a flamin'
mess
That sheila didn't take to me, I thought she'd be a gift
She's gone and changed her duty hours, and works the daylight shift
In Taumarunui, Taumarunui
Taumarunui on the Main Trunk Line.

So I'm an ordinary joker, getting old before me time
For me heart's in Taumarunui on the Main Trunk Line
Taumarunui, Taumarunui
Taumarunui on the Main Trunk Line.

Beach and bach

Boarding an NAC DC-3 at Paraparaumu aerodrome, 1951.

Fokker F27 Friendship, which began to replace the DC-3 in 1960. Later came Viscounts, and the jet aircraft with which NAC ruled the sky until 1978. Along the way it swallowed a private competitor, SPANZ (South Pacific Airlines of New Zealand), then it, too, disappeared — merged with Air New Zealand (which itself had replaced TEAL in 1965).

The first scheduled commercial flight out of New Zealand took place on 30 April 1940 when the TEAL flying-boat *Aotearoa* lifted off the Waitemata Harbour for Australia — a trip that in those days took nine hours. TEAL (Tasman Empire Airways Ltd) was then jointly owned by the governments of New Zealand, Australia and Britain. In 1961 it would become wholly New

Zealand owned. In the mid-fifties DC-6s began to replace the flying-boats and later in the same decade the DC-6 itself would begin to give way to jet-propelled Electras.

International travel, by both sea and air, was increasing steadily but it was air travel with its speed and novelty that had special allure for Kiwis going off to see the world. Flying became something that conferred status, and the symbol of this status was the TEAL flight bag. The possession of one of those grey plastic zippered bags marked its owner as a member of a special class and the bags themselves remained in circulation as work bags and the like long after the flight was over.

In 1965 the flight bag followed the TEAL company into oblivion when the

company became Air New Zealand, although a small reminder of former days survives in the identification prefix — TE — carried by Air New Zealand flights.

New Zealand has always had one of the world's lowest driving ages. It came to be commonplace for licences to be gained soon after the 15th birthday, followed in some families by the proud ownership of a second-hand 'bomb'. In country areas, of course, where there was a greater number and diversity of vehicles close to hand, farm children could be driving a lot earlier. It is a familiarity with motoring that gave rise in the sixties and early seventies to what seems in retrospect a golden age for New Zealand motor-racing, when the band of Bruce McLaren, Denny Hulme and Chris Amon raced to the top of Grand Prix competition. McLaren founded McLaren Racing which is today still among the leading race teams.

Bruce McLaren.

COOPER BRISTOL
...(G. Britain)

*T*he cars we loved and drove for the greater part of this century — including the Rovers, Triumphs, Morrises and Austins — had, in many respects, less to do with reflecting New Zealand's British heritage and more to do with the trade preferences worked out by Great Britain and its Dominions at the 1932 Imperial Conference in Ottawa. Up until then in this country American models had dominated sales, among them Fords, Chryslers, Chevrolets, Hudsons, Buicks, Pontiacs and other marques. But the Ottawa agreement made the previously higher priced British cars more than competitive. The works of Detroit gave way to those of Cowley. The roads hummed to cars with wonderful names like Vanguard Spacemaster, Morris Minor, Humber Hawk, Triumph Mayflower, Vauxhall Wyvern and Zephyr.

In addition, from the late 1940s, this country shared a fascination with its cousins across the Tasman for the first wholly Australian car, the Holden. Roomy, powerful, rugged and well priced, the Holden — and perhaps its FB, EH and EK models especially — came to be part of Kiwi life, as much at home down on the farm and in provincial market towns as in suburbia.

The dominance of British Commonwealth cars began to be undermined in the mid 1960s with the trickling in of imports from Japan, a trickle that became a veritable flood a few years later when import controls were lifted. Today, it is Mitsubishi, Honda, Toyota and Nissan — cars with less redolent names and a sameness of appearance, but much more efficiency — that whisk us to work and play. But not entirely. If you've ever thought that there still seems to be an awful lot of Morris Minors on the road, you're right. More here, in fact, per head of population than anywhere else on earth.

Another marque that made its mark on the New Zealand motoring subculture was the Ford. The Ford Motor Company began New Zealand operations in Lower Hutt in 1936. The first model off the production line was the V8 coupe of that year, a great car and still very desirable today. With the advent of the Second World War, car production was halted and all resources were devoted to the war effort. Instead military transporters, armoured cars and artillery tractors were produced for defence.

Zephyr.

Consul.

Zodiac.

138

The Holden is the marque that more than any other is associated with New Zealand driving. Designed as 'Australia's Own Car', the Holden quickly adopted New Zealand as well following its release here in 1954. Since then some 300,000 Holdens of all types have found their way onto our roads. On 31 January 1957 the first New Zealand-made Holdens — FE series — went on sale.

A rare find today is a leftover vehicle from the mid fifties to early sixties which still sports a blue-lensed light on its roof. A provision in the traffic regulations of that period required all motor vehicles towing a trailer or carrying an unusually wide load to display a blue light, mounted high, centrally and directed forward, to warn oncoming traffic.

HOLDEN
now proving its rugged dependability in New Zealand

'A rare find . . .'.

In 1950 Ford UK launched their new range of 'Five Star Cars' which were to enjoy huge popularity on the New Zealand market when assembly of complete knocked down (CKD) units began at the Seaview Plant in Lower Hunt from 1952 onwards. Scores of thousands of New Zealanders flocked to dealers' showrooms at the launching of the Five Star range, which included the four-cylinder Consul and the six-cylinder Zephyr and Zodiac. Commonly known as the Zephyr 6, the Mark I Zephyr became famous when in January 1953 one was driven to victory in that year's Monte Carlo Rally. Its power and road-handling qualities soon made it a favourite of local bodgies and their hoon progeny on our roads. But this is a tarnished image that is now receding as the cars are better restored and driven more sedately.

Production of the Mark I Consul and Zephyr ceased in 1957 with the release of the Mark 2 range of the three models. Again these were displayed in showrooms to high interest. Ford Australia went one better and added a special ute version of the Consul and Zephyr for use in the Aussie outback. A Mark 3 range followed in 1962 — now without the Consul — and a final Mark 4 range of Zephyrs and Zodiacs was introduced locally in late 1966. Although this range was continued until 1972, it faced increasing competition from Australian Fords — Fairmonts and Falcons — and Holden, and never enjoyed the sales success of its predecessors.

Once driven, never forgotten — the ubiquitous 'Morrie'. Dubbed by Lord Nuffield, the car's manufacturer, 'a poached egg', the Morris Minor is a car that most of us have either owned or driven at some stage in our lives.

Its designer, Alec Issigonis, was the last of the back-of-an-old-envelope brigade whose liking for a commonsense, endearing design of motorcar was shared by the millions who bought and drove the Minor during its more than two decades of production. First released in 1948, the Morrie became a huge commercial success due to its reliability, economy, power and well-proportioned friendly shape. And nearly 20 years after its demise the memory of its special character lingers still. There was, for example, the distinctive noise through the gears, not to mention the unique

Beach and bach

smell of the interior, the latter apparently to do with the leatherette used in the upholstery or the glue used to stick it on.

In 1960 the Morris Minor became the first British car to achieve one million sales. Its manufacturers contributed to the celebrations with a publicity release which, while reflecting the current interest in things extraterrestrial, was somewhat overdone in trying to make a connection between the two: 'The production of 1,000,000 vehicles of a common design is a feat never before achieved by British Industry, the magnitude of which can be exemplified by saying that if all the units which have left the production lines at Cowley were spaced at intervals of 407 yards 11½ inches the first would rest in Oxfordshire and

the millionth would have its wheels on the moon.'

An estimated 1.6 million Minors were made and of this number about 60,000 to 70,000 found their way to New Zealand roads, initially imported fully built-up but later assembled here at the Dominion Motors (later NZ Motor Corporation) plant in Newmarket, Auckland. Production of the saloon ended worldwide in 1970, but vans and utilities for the local market continued to be assembled here until four years later. Of the estimated quarter-million Morries still on the road around the world, some 10,000 or so are still on the go here.

Competition in Britain during the late 1930s and through the 1940s to produce cheap, modestly priced family transport saw continuing competition

between the Austin-Morris products and Ford of England. While they never had the mass appeal of the Cowley cars, the small 8 and 10 hp Fords were nevertheless a popular source of family transport both in the UK and here. The first of the many models was the Model Y in 1932. The late 1930s saw the release of the first Anglia and Prefect designs.

Unique to New Zealand is the exclusive pedestrian phase at some city intersections. In this the lights go red to stop cars in all directions, allowing pedestrians to cross diagonally as well as at right angles. This, the 'Barnes Dance' as it is known, is named for its originator, a New York police commissioner of the 1930s. But that city didn't retain the idea for very long when it was realised the system was at odds with the need for continuing traffic flow, especially on busy city centre streets. In New Zealand, however, with its relatively relaxed traffic flows, the Barnes Dance is a curiosity we've retained.

A fascinating episode in personal mobility began in the early 1960s when the country experienced something of a scooter boom. Two-wheeled motorised transport had been dominated here by British bikes, but the development in the late fifties of smaller-engined mopeds and scooters, by mainly European manufacturers, led to a keen demand locally for their products. Italian, British, French and Japanese bikes with names like Puch, Rabbit, Tigress and Vespa began to appear on New Zealand roads, but perhaps most famous was the NZeta.

A local version of the Czechoslovakian Cezeta, the NZeta was assembled from knocked-down Cezeta machines to which a substantial percentage of local content, in the form of batteries, tyres and paint was added — in order to comply with import regulations then in force. The result was similar in virtually all respects to the parent machine. The first NZeta was released in 1960. Three years, and 3500 bikes, later the import and assembly company ceased production.

A promotional photograph taken to launch the NZeta.

The cars we loved and drove.

Beach and bach

Edward Fristrom's 'Pohutukawa' is an evocative image of coastal New Zealand in the summer.

Given that the farthest you can ever be from the sea in New Zealand is something like 130 km (in fact it is the residents of Garston, Southland, who must travel furthest for a day at the beach) and, further, that the great majority of the country's population lives little more than 10 km from the coast, it's only natural that The Beach should assume such a large role in our lives. Add to that the rich profusion of bathing beaches we enjoy along a coastline of over 6000 km, and it's little wonder that the Christmas holidays see a lemming-like migration from our cities and towns.

Traditionally schooling and commerce have ground to a halt from around the middle of December and not started up again until late in January (or the first week in February in the case of schools).

From their suburban homes New Zealanders head east or west to settle along the coast like so many migratory birds, making their temporary homes in tents, caravans and baches. For a society already greatly egalitarian, the beach is the final levelling, where labourers and executives, farming folk and townies blend together in a confusion of jandals, shorts and t-shirts, togs and towelling hats.

The New Zealand coastline is a network of inlets and rocky coves, shelly bays and long sweeps of smooth, sandy beach. These latter vary enormously, both in the colour of the sand and the nature of the swimming itself. The west coast beachgoer has at times to endure the intense heat of black iron-sand, which means hopping from towel to

towel if footwear has been forgotten. On the east coast conditions are far less arduous and wild, and sparkling white sands cover more gently shelving beaches.

The popularity of swimming in the sea and the cult of the beach are of comparatively recent origin, taking hold in the last 100 years or so. At the end of the 19th century the seaside, which up until then had been largely ignored as a place of recreation — rather it was in the main the preserve of fishermen and others whose livelihoods were entwined with the sea — became fashionable. At first there were bathing machines and cloaks clasped about the shoulders to keep modestly clad figures from public view. But gradually society's strictures on the matter relaxed...up to a point.

Nowhere in New Zealand is far from the sea and as a consequence New Zealanders have perhaps a greater awareness of the connections between land and sea. In both Maori and European history there are a number of recorded instances of benign contact between humans and the sea's friendly denizens, but none of more note in recent times than Opo, the dolphin of Opononi. While an earlier contact with a dolphin — Pelorus Jack — took place over a much longer period — 24 years, in fact, spanning the turn of the century, compared with just a few months in the case of Opo — the latter's impact during the summer of 1955-56 was much greater.

Like Pelorus Jack, who delighted in accompanying Wellington-Nelson steamships for part of their journey, Opo's first love was also messing about with boats. But she soon came closer inshore, playing among swimmers, leaping out of the water, tossing a beach ball and allowing herself to be handled.

In 1891 one local borough council declared itself as 'not in favour' of swimming at all by women or girls, and even limited the hours that males could bathe — before 8 am and after 6 pm only. It was a losing battle, however. Not only was the council unable to enforce any swimming curfew, but it also found it impossible to compel male swimmers to use the accepted form of bathing-suit or, in fact, any bathing-suit at all.

A greater problem was sharks. On the evidence of press reports from around the turn of the century, schools of sharks were then common close in to the shore. This was due no doubt to the negligible disturbance of the waters by powered craft then and the limited commercial fishing of inshore fisheries.

Writing in the 1880s about Auckland's North Shore, E. W. Payton described the area as having '...one or two long stretches of beautiful sandy shore...but these cannot unfortunately be used much for bathing as the water is infested with sharks...'.

From the 1880s through the 1930s it was mostly trains and buses that conveyed New Zealanders to the seaside, but the advent of the motorcar resulted in the opening up of otherwise inaccessible parts of the coast to day-trippers and holidaymakers. Accompanying this was the institution of that little slice of heaven by the sea called the bach. Through to the 1960s the humble bach, usually a utilitarian habitation made of car-case, fibrolite or board-and-batten, mushroomed along the coastline. With the effects of inflation

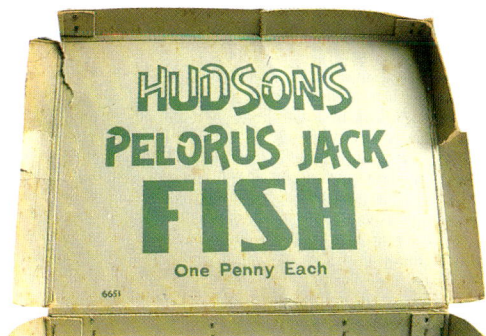

from the late 1960s, however, the bach has become an unaffordable luxury for the average worker, and the once-humble bolt-hole is being increasingly replaced by the kind of houses, with all mod cons, we were once happy to leave back in town.

Beach and bach

Messing about in small boats is second nature to most New Zealanders.

Yachting in particular finds its way into the lives of many young Kiwis when they are just knee-high — and more often than not it's aboard a P-class that they first learn their starboards from their ports.

The ubiquitous P-class — it would be difficult to find any top-class New Zealand yachtie who hasn't sailed in one — was designed by Harry Highet, who launched his prototype on New Year's Day, 1920, at Onerahi Bay, Whangarei. Within a few years the P-class had proved sufficiently popular for a national championship in its class to be inaugurated. These races continue today under the auspices of the Tauranga Yacht Club to whom Harry Highet gave control of the design. As a small boat that could be confidently sailed by youngsters, the P-class has proved ideal.

The cult of the beach — sun, surf, swimming and sea breeze — is one that is shared on both sides of the Tasman. For many years summers at the beach were spent clad in a pair of Speedo togs, the label launched in Australia in the mid 1920s as the 'all-Aussie cossie'. Like the first Ford car — available in any colour as long as it was black — the original Speedo cotton-knit swimsuit was available only in navy blue.

'The all-Aussie cossie' — Speedo togs.

Sadly the toheroa has now gone the way of the *4d* pint of milk and our once-excellent postal service . . . for different reasons, but gone all the same. And it's unlikely that we shall ever see again the kind of open season that once existed on the country's west coast beaches up until the early 1970s. In those days there'd be hundreds of cars out on the hard low-tide sands of Auckland and Northland beaches in particular as groups of families and friends reverted to hunter-gatherers, using wooden spades or sticks or simply bare hands to dig down into the wet black sand in search of this delicacy.

The toheroa is a member of the clam family and when eaten — particularly as a soup — has a memorable taste. But nowadays you'll have to make do with tuatua or pipi instead, both of which are still in abundance. Massively declining

Breakfast during a camping trip, late 1930s. The cereal was of course Weet-Bix.

toheroa numbers through the 1960s due to a combination of damaging gathering practices (thousands of the shellfish were crushed by car wheels and feet), overfishing, and an increase in predation by crabs, resulted in the 'closed season' signs going up. And they look like staying there for some time yet.

Hunter-gatherers at Muriwai, 1963.

In the Sticks

In the sticks

Loading cream cans, Wainuiomata, 1950s.

No single activity has affected the physical and economic face of New Zealand as much as farming. Early settlers from Britain came to convert New Zealand into a farm to supply the mother-country with produce but were not our first farmers: New Zealand had already sustained a basic Polynesian agriculture for some 800 years. The ancestors of the Maori had brought with them a number of crops, but only the kumara was to survive. Fortunately the new land was well stocked with fish, birds, berries and fern roots to otherwise support its first agriculturalists.

With the Europeans came new crops, and the potato supplanted the kumara. Soon the Maori had a healthy industry provisioning the whaling and trading ships that were visiting the far North in

increasing numbers, and later the emergent European settlements in the Auckland area. It was the growing of wheat at which the Maori excelled. In the Waikato and Bay of Plenty thousands of acres were grown, later to be processed in Maori-owned mills. The produce was brought to Auckland in small coastal vessels and canoes, and traded for sought-after European goods.

Not only did the Maori feed the populace of Auckland in the 1840s and '50s, but they were probably the main producers of New Zealand's food exports across the Tasman as well. But this agricultural pre-eminence, based on energy and adaptation, ended abruptly. As a result of the Land Wars the Maori holdings were confiscated.

In the mid 1800s the New Zealand

landscape was about to undergo some major agricultural transformations. The first of these resulted from the discovery of gold in Otago, which in turn led to a population explosion in the province. Fortunately Otago's climate and massive acreage were well equipped to supply wheat for daily bread. Soon some of these pastures were accommodating sheep, and produced the first real fortunes made off the land in New Zealand.

At the same time in the North Island land-hungry settlers were converting virgin forest to grazing by way of the axe and match. Valuable stands of timber were often simply incinerated. Between the charred stumps and logs grass seed was sown so that stock could graze and a return could be obtained from the land.

For the greater part of the last 150 years farming has played a major role in the nation's economy. Neither the increased industrialisation of the last 30 years, nor the attempts during the present decade to turn the country into some kind of Hong Kong of the South Pacific have been sufficient to put even a dent in agriculture's pre-eminent position. And, despite (or perhaps, *because* of) an increasing urbanisation, many of us continue to feel strongly the pull of the land — an attachment to an idyll of rolling farmland dotted with sheep, a red-roofed farmhouse set about with hydrangeas and daffodils in the spring, hand-fed lambs in the house paddock, a couple of border collies and a Fordson or Massey Ferguson at the ready.

The stereotypical New Zealander is, to many, still a sheepfarmer whose pioneer attributes of self-reliance and

practical skills still count for something, even half a dozen generations on. The reality is of course a little different, but proof that the concept is a popular one is provided by the huge following that once attended Fred Dagg and that today pays homage to the exploits at *Footrot Flats*. The creation of cartoonist Murray Ball, *Footrot Flats* was first published here in 1975. Today it is syndicated throughout New Zealand and Australia (more than 120 newspapers), as well as appearing in Finland, Sweden

and Norway, among other places.

With what has been described as an appeal to 'cowpat patriotism' *Footrot Flats* has been the big popular publishing phenomenon of the last 10 years — a spectacular success that has spawned hugely successful annuals (the biggest selling books on *both* sides of the Tasman), a stage show, a film and a host of merchandising. All thanks to a recipe that blends the realities and fantasies of rural life with a Dog struggling to make some sense out of it all.

© 1987 Diogenes Designs Ltd

Beginning as modest toeholds carved out of the bush, these farms grew steadily, nourished by ashes from the ancient domain of Tane. Further stimulated by the possibilities opened up by the frozen export trade, our sheep and dairy industries soon overtook grain-growing in importance. But there was a price to pay: land now denuded of its cover was vulnerable to the elements, and the ugly scars of erosion crept across the hills.

In this raw new land, such as New Zealand was then, farming was for most a tough, demanding life — perseverance and sheer hard work was called for. Many young New Zealanders, returning from the First World War, were balloted land and thus broke in a new generation of back–country sheep farms. Some didn't make it but those who hung on

became the veritable backbone of the country's economy. They were perhaps able to retire, eventually, with some financial reward for their years of service.

The geography of the New Zealand farm has at its centre the farmhouse. This differs little from that used by the town-dweller apart from perhaps the greater number of gumboots and wet-weather gear cluttering the back porch of the farmer. But inside, there was — until comparatively recent times — another reliable distinction: the rural housewife, hardly straying from the stove, keeping up a constant supply of cooking and baking to satisfy hearty round-the-clock appetites. Such kitchen activity demanded a well-stocked pantry, and there was invariably a cat or two to

contain the mice this attracted.

The farmhouse was generally a relaxed and comforting stop for a myriad of callers, from distant 'next-door' neighbours to stock and station agents and seasonal workers. There was always a fresh brew of tea and a ready packet of 'Park Drive' and its accompanying Zig Zag papers. Perhaps in a less formal part of the dining room where work clothes were permitted there would be a well-worn sofa littered with issues of the pink-covered *Weekly News*, and *Farmer* magazines. The wireless was nearby, for essential weather forecasts and wool prices, or perhaps the dividends from the second leg at Te Rapa. Above the smoke and chatter there was the persistent morse-like ringing of the telephone, its party line providing an essential

In the sticks

First made in 1937 by John McKendrick, a tailor, the Swanndri has become part of New Zealand fashion, the original rugged garment synonymous with bushworking and farming.

The original 'swanni', a dark green bushshirt, was quickly adopted by bushmen and farmers for its warmth and proof against showers — qualities deriving from its 100 percent pure wool and a special process that sees the woven cloth shrunk to increase its moisture-resistance.

From the original garment there has now been developed a line of jackets and shirts for leisure and work wear, sold here and exported around the world.

From the start these garments have been produced in the small Taranaki town of Waitara. The mis-spelt trade name is deliberate, these days anyway: in the beginning it was a simple slip of the pen.

Second only to the 'swanni' in popularity, the black oilskin parkha was once a common outdoor garment. 'Was' because the last decade or so has seen its decline against more convenient synthetic versions. While never achieving the fashion heritage status here that the similar Aussie 'Drizabone' coat has been accorded in that country, the oilskin parkha was still the outer garment most people wore tramping, on the sidelines watching a rugby game, at spring stock sales. It

John McKendrick.

was a garment that exuded character, in the aromatic scent of the oil and waxes used to waterproof its cotton fabric, and, when wet, from the gently steaming checked flannel lining.

community link.

Beyond the family hearth was a scattering of smaller buildings. Regularly visited was the outside dunny, whose basic gravity-assisted long-drop design was increasingly replaced by the inside flushing variety from the 1940s. Nearby were the washhouse and other sheds for storage of home-grown fruit and vegetables, and also the separator. This centrifugal device was, more often than not, an Alfa-Laval, popular models of which in this country were the Viola and Daisy. Swinging the handle to remove the cream from the milk was often the responsibility of junior members of the family, a job that could be eased with a little Lubriline or Lister separator oil.

Further afield may have been a modest whare or temporary quarters for itinerant workers, and a small community of dog kennels. These essential farmhands were given to nocturnal outbursts when disturbed, their chains rattling against their corrugated-iron shelters. Otherwise, the only sound of the country was the morepork, or native owl, calling its name from high up in the trees.

The economic heart of the farm is its cowshed or woolshed. The first is a strictly functional concrete-floored structure that sees use, morning and evening, every day of the year. The other is traditionally a larger weatherboarded edifice in an architectural genre of its own and the scene of the annual wool clip. At this time of year distant paddocks run white with woolly sheep — and a few startled goats — being

mustered towards the yards by diligent dogs.

Conveniently spaced floorboards in the woolshed allow the passage of millions of black bouncing droppings. Everywhere else, timber surfaces have a dark glow from the buffing by greasy wool. The shearing itself is repetitive and relentless: the distant roar of the generator, the buzz of shears, baa-ing of sheep and the banging of sprung doors as another victim is dragged in. Nearby, a credit to ingenuity, is the giant woolpress used to condense the day's take into bales.

Early farms were isolated in more ways than one. The homestead may have been built from timber dragged from the nearest road across country on a horse-drawn sled. At first the horse provided the only link with the outside world, but

later a gig enabled the whole family to venture out in comparative comfort. A major excursion was the regular trip to the nearest town, often a day-long outing. This enabled the stocking up of provisions, visiting the Dalgety's man, and perhaps a small investment with the local bookie. But such trips needed to be planned carefully, for sudden downpours could cause rivers to rise and make fords impassable.

When internal combustion hit the back-roads of New Zealand, the early cars were usually American. When their useful service was complete they were often relegated to a back paddock to commune with nature. Some were rediscovered years later as rusty skeletons and restored to their former glory by enthusiasts. Luckier vehicles

spent their twilight years up on blocks, stationary but powering a home-made sawmill, perhaps converting trimmings from the macrocarpa wind-break into fuel for the kitchen range. After the Second World War, English cars were more plentiful in these parts, and Vauxhalls, for example, were popular with farmers. The arrival of such a vehicle was often presaged by a dust cloud on the horizon, whipped up along the rutted papa-surfaced roads.

A feature of country life is its community spirit. Isolation means that families need to look to their neighbours for assistance — be it manual or medical. A local school would be at the hub, its visiting teacher boarding with a local family, and its hall doubling for social events. But even after an evening of

boisterous Gay Gordons and a hearty supper there were still cows to milk the next morning. Prominent on the social calendar were the A & P shows, with displays of skills as diverse as wood-chopping, highland dancing and pig rearing — always a good excuse for a family picnic.

New Zealand's dairy industry has, of course, stimulated innumerable supply industries, among them some of New Zealand's largest companies. In 1886 Alexander Harvey and his three sons began making milk and cream cans in the loft of a corrugated-iron shed in Durham Street, Auckland. Business boomed and soon demanded bigger premises. In 1914 the company's 'RV' (presumably 'Harvey' with a dropped 'H') seamless milk and cream cans

In the sticks

'Anchor' is a trademark that has long been associated with exports of New Zealand dairy products. It is internationally known for quality and reliability, and perhaps a certain muscularity in the way it has achieved success worldwide. Appropriately the symbol is derived from the anchor tattoo worn by one of the workers on the Waikato farm of Henry Reynolds who gave this name to his butter in 1886. Reynolds later sold his creamery interest to the New Zealand Dairy Association along with the brand and in 1919 the National Co-operative Dairy Company took it over. Today the Anchor label continues to identify quality exports to a billion-dollar world market.

ANCHOR BUTTER
World-wide distribution

THE Anchor "Sailor Boy" travels the Seven Seas bringing to discriminating buyers his packets of dainty butter, outstanding in flavour, purity and health building properties

PRODUCED BY
THE NEW ZEALAND DAIRY
CO LTD.

SOLE EXPORT AGENTS
AMALGAMATED DAIRIES LTD., ANZAC AV., AUCKLAND, & EMPIRE BLDG., TOOLEY ST., LONDON, S.E.1.
AGENCIES THROUGHOUT THE WORLD

New Zealand's 60 million sheep (give or take a few million) are spread out in around 25,000 farms which occupy in total two-fifths of the country's total land area. On all of them the rhythm of the farming year is similar. Lambing gives way to shearing, tupping, crutching and back to lambing. Shearing was traditionally an annual event, sometime in midsummer, but many farmers today shear twice, in July as well as January. It's a skill that Kiwi shearers have honed finely. Godfrey Bowen first put New Zealand shearing on the world map in 1953 with a record nine-hour-day tally of 456 sheep.

DOMINION DIP
A NEW ZEALAND PRODUCT

boasted three coats of pure tin and 'no seams or crevices for dirt or microbes to lodge in'.

About this time tin-printing began, which made Alex Harvey and Sons even more of a household name. By 1950 the company had relocated at Mt Wellington and in 1983 absorbed the Auckland timber and joinery giant, Henderson and Pollard. Like Harvey's, this company, too, once had agricultural connections. In its early days it produced wooden butter churns, and later built wooden trams for Auckland. Perhaps its most unusual contract was the supply of some 100 timber and hessian Hurricane fighter aeroplanes and Hudson bombers, intended to fool the Japanese during the Second World War.

In recent times New Zealand farming has witnessed alarming changes. The oil shocks of the early 1970s, Britain's entry into the EEC, spiralling inflation and crippling interest rates and the rationalisation of the local freezing industry brought to an end an age of seemingly perpetual prosperity. In need of new markets and in response to the demands of changing eating habits, New Zealand agriculture has had to diversify. Subsidies have been lifted and farmers have had a real taste of market forces. These shake-ups and re-adjustments have been ruinous for some, but farming has recovered from such body-blows before. New Zealand may no longer be regarded as a food-basket for Britain but agriculture will always be the backbone of its economy.

Success, even survival as a farmer in New Zealand has often been allied to an ability to make-do and improvise. Over the years *The Weekly News* published thousands of original time, labour, and money-saving hints, thoughtfully compiled by 'Handy Andy'.

Certain aspects of the farm were always open to improvement, especially gates. Easily the most celebrated — and basic — solution in this respect was the Taranaki gate, part of the vernacular by at least the 1930s. But Handy Andy had better ideas, such as a counter-weighted self-closing variety. Alternatively 'improved' gate catches could be fashioned from an old dray shaft, hinges from old flat files, and a gate-stop from a discarded rabbit trap. Even an old iron bedstead was suggested as a potential farm gate with a touch of class. But it

Sheep Breeds at a Glance

The six sheep types
most numerous on
New Zealand farms:

Merino

Coopworth

New Zealand Halfbred

Corriedale

New Zealand Romney

Perendale

Corriedale — 5 million. Dual-purpose meat and wool. Mainly Canterbury, Otago and Marlborough lowlands.

Merino — 1.3 million. The dominant breed in New Zealand during the 19th century. Now mainly rugged South Island high country where merino thrive on high-altitude native grasses.

New Zealand Halfbred — 2.4 million. Dual-purpose breed with emphasis on wool. Mainly South Island foothills.

New Zealand Romney — 29 million. Dual-purpose with equal emphasis on meat and wool. Widespread throughout New Zealand.

Perendale — 11 million. Dual-purpose, with equal emphasis on meat and wool. Hill country throughout New Zealand.

Coopworth — 11.5 million. Dual-purpose breed with equal emphasis on meat and wool production. Lowland and hill country throughout New Zealand.

In the sticks

While most corrugated iron ends up on house roofs, shed walls or fences, some of it achieves a more artful end. A lack of success hitching rides during his travels led artist Jeff Thomson to quit putting his thumb out and instead take up walking. The result of his ambulatory travels through rural New Zealand has been a keen appreciation of things rustic, in particular rural mailboxes and the ways in which corrugated iron is used on farms.

Thomson began producing his own cut and rivetted constructions and it is perhaps for these marvellous inventions that he is now best known. Ranging from a family of corrugated iron elephants to scores of cows (the New Zealand embassy in Canberra is home to a small

herd which graze the diplomatic grass of its front lawn), typewriters and motor-mowers their fusion of fun and Kiwi improvisation provoke a consistently enthusiastic response.

was a home-made bell that illustrates rural recycling at its best. This 'resonant and tuneful' device cunningly combined the handle off an old car tyre pump and the bowl of a discarded separator. The clapper consisted of a large steel nut on the end of a short length of dog chain, and presumably the result could successfully summon children to dinner and farmhands to smoko.

While New Zealand farmers have always exhibited the technical resourcefulness their calling demands, not all innovations were directly applicable to farming. One South Canterbury farmer has passed into history for his particular genius with early aviation. It was around the turn of the century that Richard Pearce, farming in the small country district of Waitohi

near Timaru, first became interested in heavier-than-air flying machines. Although little was recorded at the time, evidence has shown that Pearce began aeroplane construction in 1899 with a two-cylinder air-cooled engine. His flying machine of bamboo and linen followed, the puller propellor made from metal salvaged from sheep-dip drums. It has been suggested that Pearce may have first tried to fly his monoplane — unsuccessfully, due to insufficient power — as early as 1902, from the road in front of his farm.

Pearce then developed a large engine and, according to some eyewitness reports, made successful take-offs between early 1903 and early 1904. If so, the first of these would predate the more famous flights of Orville and

Wilbur Wright by several months. It seems more likely, however, that his first flight was in March 1904, which is nonetheless remarkable. The remains of Pearce's two planes are displayed in Auckland at the Museum of Transport and Technology, along with other of his inventions.

More than just the gauge most commonly used in farm fencing, 'Number 8' has come to be synonymous with Kiwi versatility and innovation. In carving an existence out of the bush — forming farms for grazing and cropping — European settlers depended upon good fences. No. 8 gauge wire came to be strung over New Zealand farms by the thousands of miles. The uses for No. 8 went beyond just fencing, however. Lengths of the galvanised wire were put to a hundred and one uses around the farm and home, including replacement bucket handles, tent pegs and hooks.

Another source of raw material on farms was the ubiquitous 4-gallon kerosene tin. These square-sided tins were, in the days before petrol pumps, the form in which motorcar benzine, or petrol, came. Similarly kerosene, used to fuel heaters and cookers and for a myriad of

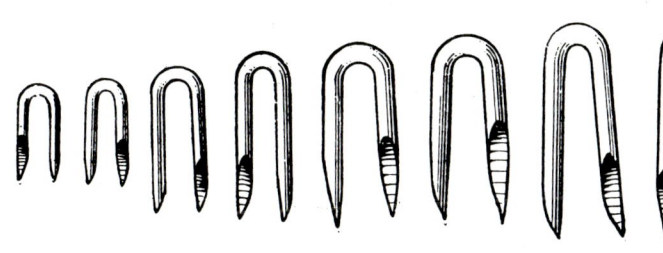

cleaning jobs from windows to linoleum floors. With a piece of No. 8 and the kero tin there wasn't much you couldn't do or make. Rural recorder Jim Henderson once published a list he'd received which detailed more than 30 applications of the kero tin, from the basic bucket (with No. 8 wire handle), to cake tins, roasting pans and nesting boxes to ashpans, chimneys and a portable toilet.

GALVANISED FENCING STAPLES: ACTUAL SIZES.

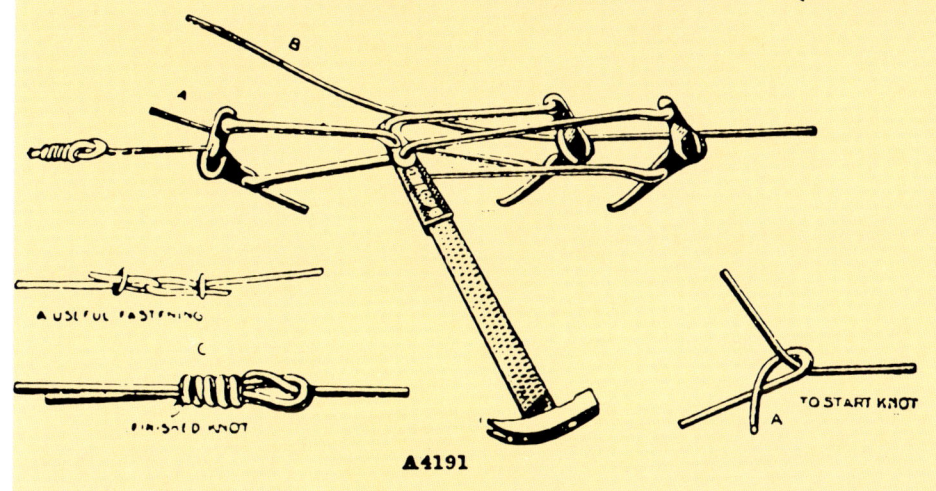

Illustration Credits

The following list identifies the copyright ownership and, where applicable, the source of items appearing in the photographs. Those illustrations and items not specifically identified are from the collections of the authors.

Abbreviations:

t = top	NZH = New Zealand Herald
b = bottom	AIM = Auckland Institute & Museum
l = left	ATL = Alexander Turnbull Library
r = right	NM = National Museum
c = centre	

Page **10** NZH; **12** *The Dominion;* **14** (l) polish tin the collection of Nicholas Kiwi (Australia), (r) Nicholas Kiwi (Australia); **15** (l) Nicholas Kiwi (Australia), (tr and c) NZH, (br) Rod Morris; (t) NZH; **17** (t and b) Geoffrey Short; **18** poppy the collection of AIM, (l) ATL (G 13460); **19** (l) ATL (C 24092), (r) Rod Morris; **20** (r) NM, (b) medal the collection of AIM; **21** (c) Rod Morris, (br) Rugby Museum Society of NZ Inc.; **22** (l) periscope the collection of Ron Palenski, (c) ATL National Publicity Studios Collection (F 42761); **23** (l) NZH; **24** NZH; **25** NZH; **26** NZH; **28** (l) ATL (F 18662), (c and r) Royal NZ Plunket Society; **29** (t) ATL National Publicity Studios Collection (F 33847), (r) Royal NZ Plunket Society; **30** (l) ATL (G 23991), (c) ATL (G 21703); **31** Department of Education; **32** (l and r) ATL National Publicity Studios Collection (F 33808, F 105154); **33** (l) Department of Health, (c) ATL Health Dept Collection (83959); **34** (l) ATL Making New Zealand Collection (F 2461MNZ), (r) NZH; **36** (tr) Butland Industries Ltd, (b) ATL; **37** (tl) collection NZ Co-operative Dairy Company; **38** (b) NZH; **39** (b) TVNZ; **40** (l, tr and br) the collection of Barry Young; **41** (tl and c) the collection of Barry Young; **42** (tr and r) collection of Joan Ramsey; **43** toys the collection of Joan Ramsey; **44** (r) Tip Top Company Ltd; **45** (r) ATL Gordon Burt Collection; **46** (c and r) TT2 wrappers the collection of Tip Top Company Ltd; **48** (t) Tip Top Company Ltd; **49** (l) NZH; **50** (r) collection of Jenny Devine; **52** ATL Gordon Burt Collection (F 36689); **54** (l) ATL McAllister Collection, (r) ATL Dyson Album (F 14985); **55** (l) ATL (G 11180); **56** (l) ATL (G 19105); **57** *Brett's Colonists' Guide;* **59** (r) ATL Whitehead Collection (G 4732); **61** (l) ATL Making New Zealand Collection (F 2167MNZ); **62** (l) NZH, (r) 'A nicely mown lawn' David Mealing; **64** (l) Steven La Plant, (c and r) collection of Yates NZ Ltd; **65** all photos collection of Yates NZ Ltd; **67** illustration of paspallum from *An Introduction to the Grasses of New Zealand,* H. H. Allen, Government Printer (1936); **69** Masport Ltd; **70** both illustrations the collection of Flemings and Co. Ltd; **74** (b) ATL (126475); **75** (l) ATL (138048); **78** NZH; **86** (t) collection of Unilever Ltd; **87** (l) ATL Gordon Burt Collection (F 36689), (r) Grant Sheehan; **88** (l) NM (C 2529), (r) NZH; **90** (l) Ford Motor Company, (r) NZH; **91** (t) NZH; **92** (t) cover the collection of Bluebird Foods Ltd; **93** photos the collection of Bluebird Foods Ltd; **94** (t) Bluebird Foods Ltd; **96** (t) label the collection of J. Watties Canneries Ltd; **97** (t and b) J. Watties Canneries Ltd; **98** NZH; **100** (l) ATL (C 9205), (br) ATL (G 10310); **101** (l) Rugby Press, (r) Canterbury International; **102** (l) Stephen Robinson, (r) NZH; **103** (l) NM (C 2653); **104** (c) NZH, (b) ATL (G 22979); **105** (t) NZH, (r) Grant Sheehan, (bl) NZH; **106** (t and b) NZH; **107** labels the collection of Dominion Breweries; **108** (l) ATL (124283), (r) ATL (124320); **109** (l) ATL (126983), (c and tr) collection of Dominion Breweries; **110** labels the collection of Corbans Wines Ltd; **111** (l) ATL (126983); **112** (r) collection of Oasis Industries; **116** (r) NM (C 2389); **118** (l) Grant Sheehan, (r) NZH; **119** Dennis Turner; **120** NZH; **121** (l and c) collection of Philip Warren, (r) NZH; **122** (l and r) collection of Philip Warren; **123** (l, c and r) NZH, (far r) collection of Philip Warren; **124** NZH; **125** (l and r) NZH; **126** NZH; **127** NZH; **128** (t and c) NZH; **129** (b) ATL (112278), (t) NZH; **130** ATL (C 9206); **132** NZH; **133** (l) ATL (126386), (r) ATL (126093); **134** ATL (557); **135** (r) ATL National Studios Collection (F 40507); **136** (r) ATL National Studios Collection (F 40512), (br) bag the collection of Air New Zealand; **137** (l) ATL (C 9209); **138** collection of the Ford Motor Company of NZ; **139** (lc and lb) collection of the Ford Motor Company of NZ, (r) NZH; **140** collection of Morris Minor Car Club of New Zealand Inc.; **141** (tr) Laurie Summers Accessories Ltd, (bl) NM (C 2549); **142** (l) ATL (C 9206), (r) Auckland City Art Gallery; **143** (t) NZH; **144** (t) NM, (bl) NZH, (b) F. W. H. Short; **145** (tr) ATL (F 10114), (bl) NZH; **146** NZH; **148** (l) NZH, (r) ATL National Publicity Studios Collection (F 27360); **149** both illustrations Diogenes Designs Ltd; **150** all items the collection of Swanndri Ltd; **151** (r) ATL (126123); **153** Rod Morris; **154** (tl and tr) Jeff Thomson, (br) unknown; **155** (cr) ATL Free Lance Collection (F 104698).

The drawings on pp. 36, 104 and 111 are by Dave Gunson. Those on p. 153 are by Colin Edgerley.

Advertisements and graphics appearing throughout the book are drawn from copies of *The Weekly News,* Farmers Trading Company catalogues, and *The Mirror.* Trademarks are reprinted from *Well Made New Zealand — A Century of Trademarks* by Richard Wolfe, Heinemann Reid Publishers, 1987.

Index

Stephen Barnett and Richard Wolfe live in Auckland and share a long-time interest in New Zealand popular culture.

Stephen Barnett is a partner in the Auckland book production and publishing company Bookmakers. His previous books include *A Picture Book of Old Auckland*, *The Rubber-Band Helicopter* (with Christine Brown) and the *Those Were the Days* series (with Phillip Ridge) of pictorial compilations drawn from *The Weekly News* magazine. Richard Wolfe is curator of display at Auckland Museum. *New Zealand! New Zealand!* is his second book, the first was *Well Made New Zealand — A Century of Trademarks*.

In compiling *New Zealand! New Zealand!* the authors quickly became aware of the difficulties of compressing any survey of Kiwiana into just one book. A sequel, planned for 1991, will not only expand on the subjects raised in this book, but also delve into altogether new areas. Topics to look forward to include the definitive meat pie, how to be an All Black, rites of passage, the overseas expert, and learning to tell a saveloy from a polony.

The authors welcome comments and suggestions. Readers should address correspondence to: Stephen Barnett and Richard Wolfe, c/- PO Box 67-074, Mt Eden, Auckland.